Board Game Knits

Volume 2

Photography by RavenBlakh Photography

Sagrada Socks photography by Meyrick Harris

Book design and layout by Hannah McFarlane

Technical editing by Fiona Hamilton-MacLaren

Front and back cover images by Lola Johnson

Yarns by Third Vault Yarns, Truly Hooked, Gamecrafting and
John Arbon Textiles

Produced and printed in the United Kingdom.

Third Vault Yarns
www.thirdvaultyarns.com

All efforts have been made to ensure the patterns in this book are correct. However, if you find an error or omission, please contact Third Vault Yarns.

Board Game Knits

Volume 2

Lola Johnson

in collaboration with

Verity Castledine
Angelina Panozzo
Helena Timms
Diane Ugo

Foreword

Welcome to Volume 2 of *Board Game Knits*, in a world environment where we're feeling more separate than ever, we've all come together to create this book.

Working with friends to create Volume 2 has been a privilege, seeing all the ideas grow and keeping in touch to build this collaborative effort is a warm relief. It can't replace that fact that when we started this we were able to get together and chat and play board games, whilst now, in-person activities are trickier and we've had to find new ways to connect.

Knitting is something that a lot of us have been able to turn to, new knitters and experienced alike, our solitary pursuit, keeping our hands occupied and helping to provide some stable focus in our tumultuous world. Social knitting is still here, though it has largely moved online, which has had the wonderful benefit of bringing more of us together, our small local groups opening up globally. Sharing what we're working on through new and established platforms, and creating new networks, and reaching new people. Knitting is a celebration of creation, taking sticks and string, and building beautiful things step by step, change is a constant and growth is a given, whether we pause or rip back to fix something, we're still making something hopeful and looking towards a future.

I can only heap my praise on my fellow designers, Angie, Diane, Helena and Verity for designing beautiful patterns and following this process with me from conception to realisation, through writing, sample making, testing, tech editing and layout, all the way to this finished book.

We wouldn't have been able to do this without our sample knitters and test knitters, a huge special thank you to them. Of course the biggest thanks to all of our Kickstarter Backers, without whom this would have been a much longer road, and we wouldn't be here now without your support. You contributed to making this special.

Within this book you'll find a selection of knitting patterns inspired by some of our favourite modern-style boardgames. We've dipped our toes into different styles of gaming to bring you an assortment of accessories, from gloves and hats to socks, shawls and cowls. All levels of difficulty are represented here, from simple to more complex, and so there are projects for all sorts of knitters, and we hope that you will enjoy the range of techniques we've used within the book. We also hope that you will enjoy the little nods to the board games that we've incorporated into each pattern, and have a wonderful time knitting them.

Lola

Contents

Euro Games 2

Age of Wonders Shawl

4

Sagrada Socks

20

Settlers Mitts

26

Thematic Games 44

ApoCowlyptic

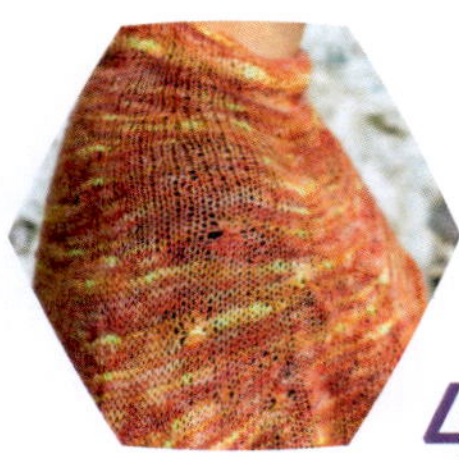

46

King of all Hats

52

Mindreaper Mitts

56

Party Games 62

Chameleon Cowl

64

Hanabi Shawl

66

Sonar Socks

82

Abbreviations, Techniques and Yarn Glossary

92

Difficulty

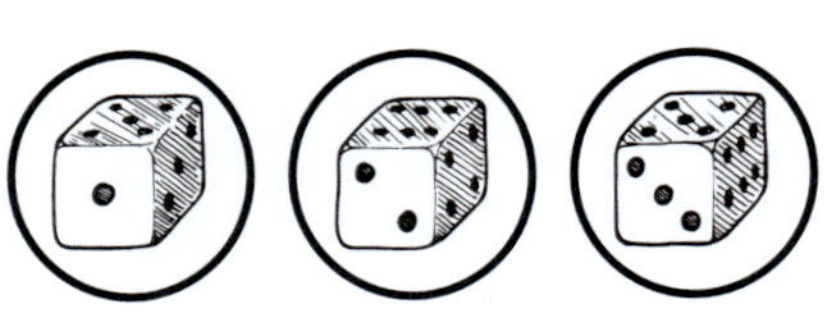

Simpler → More complex

Number of skeins

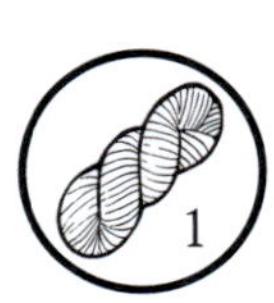

1 skein ≈ 100 g

Time

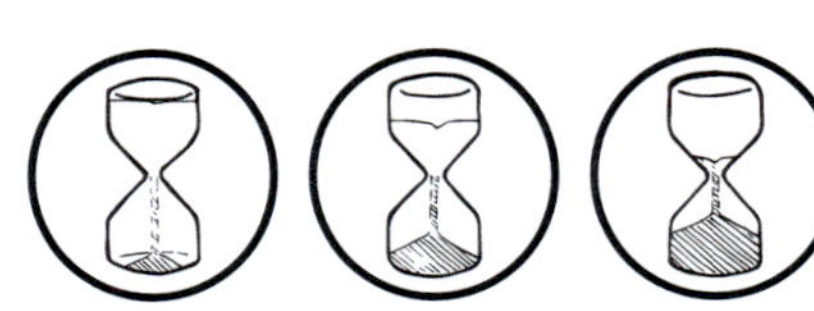

Quick knit → Long knit

Euro Games

Euro games are an increasingly popular genre of board game, and despite their name, they span across the gaming world. Originating in post-war Germany, this style of gaming allows for more indirect competition with less of a focus on warfare and conflict. Euro games have proliferated beyond Europe and this category now includes thousands of games. The games we've chosen to represent here demonstrate a variety of game mechanics, and in the patterns we've chosen to present them with a range of techniques, including texture, cables, lace and colourwork.

Age of Wonders Shawl

Lola Johnson

Building an ancient civilisation based around one of seven wonders of the world is the aim of the game in trading hands of cards over three st(ages). The Age of Wonders Shawl features 7 segments to symbolise the 7 Wonders, and 3 sections following the 3 Ages of the game, through textured stitches, cables and lace.

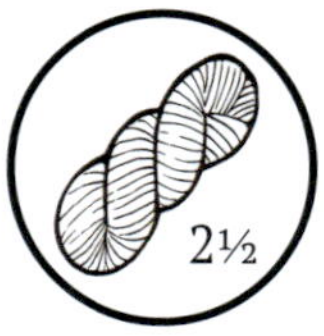

Yarn

Third Vault Yarns Companion 4 ply in *3 Ages* set, approx. 1,000 m:

Pyramids 80 m / 20 g

Temple 200 m / 50 g

Gardens 640 m / 160 g

Needle size

3.75–4 mm US 5–6 circular needles (for working flat) 100–150 cm / 40–60″ cable

Stitch markers 8–10 suggested

Size

One size

Measurements

175 cm / 67″ wide
71 cm / 28″ deep

Gauge

24 sts × 32 rows, 10 cm / 4″ in stockinette

Special stitches

DnSK: drop next stitch and k1 into the topmost bar

DnSKPK: drop next stitch and k1, p1, k1 into the topmost bar

Pyopcdd: (p1, yo, p1) in cdd sts, Slip 1 st off the needle, hold to front, slip next st purlwise, place held st on to right needle, p1, don't drop the st you purled into, then pass slipped stitches over onto your left needle, yarnover, p1 through those 3 sts, then drop those sts off the left needle.

Kyokcdd: (k1, yo, k1) in cdd sts. Slip 2 stitches as if to knit 2 together, k1, don't drop the st you knit into, pass slipped sts over onto your left needle, yarnover and knit through those 3 sts, then drop those sts off the left needle.

Kpk: (k1, p1, k1) in 1 stitch. Knit, purl and knit into the same stitch to make 3 stitches from 1.

Set up

Provisionally CO 3 sts

Knit 6 rows.

Turn work 90 degrees, yo, place marker, pick up and ptbl into the first garter nub, yo, pick up and ptbl into the second garter nub, pm, yo, pick up and knit 3 cast on sts. (11 sts)

Row 0: K4, sm, m1r, k1, m1r, k1, m1l, k1, m1l, k4. (15 sts)

When following the charts the green column of sts is the start of your repeat, for all repeats apart from the 1st repeat on a RS, which starts one stitch in from the green st, and the last repeat on a WS which ends one stitch before the green st.

Pyramids of Giza

Reverse stockinette with double moss texture

Row 1 (WS): K2, k2tog, yo, slip marker, *p1, pm*, repeat from * to * 5 (for a total of 6) times, k1, slip marker, yo, ssk, k2.

Row 2 (RS): K4, sm, p1, *k1, m1pr, sm*, repeat from * to * 5 times, sm, k4. (21 sts)

From here onwards, the markers separating the segments are not referred to, only the markers at each end.

Row 3: K2, k2tog, yo, sm, *k1, p1* repeat from * to * 5 times, k1, sm, yo, ssk, k2.

Row 4: K4, sm, p1, *k1, p1*, repeat from * to * 5 times, sm, k4.

Rows 5 & 6: Repeat rows 3 and 4.

Row 7: K2, k2tog, yo, sm, *m1l, k1, m1r, p1*, repeat from * to * 5 times, m1l, k1, m1r, sm, yo, ssk, k2. (35 sts)

Row 8: K4, sm, p3, *k1, p3*, repeat from * to * 5 times, sm, k4.

Row 9: K2, k2tog, yo, sm, *k3, p1* repeat from * to * 5 times, k3, sm, yo, ssk, k2.

Row 10: Repeat row 8.

Row 11: K2, k2tog, yo, sm, *m1l, k3, m1r, p1*, repeat from * to * 5 times, m1l, k3, m1r, sm, yo, ssk, k2. (49 sts)

Row 12: K4, sm, p5, *k1, p5*, repeat from * to * 5 times, sm, k4.

Row 13: K2, k2tog, yo, sm, *k5, p1*, repeat from * to * 5 times, k5, sm, yo, ssk, k2.

Row 14: Repeat row 12.

Row 15: K2, k2tog, yo, sm, *m1l, k5, m1r, p1*, repeat from * to * 5 times, m1l, k5, m1r, sm, yo, ssk, k2. (63 sts)

Row 16: K4, sm, p7, *k1, p7*, repeat from * to * 5 times, sm, k4.

Row 17: K2, k2tog, yo, sm, *k7, p1* repeat from * to * 5 times, k7, sm, yo, ssk, k2.

Row 18: Repeat row 16.

Row 19: K2, k2tog, yo, sm, *m1l, k3, p1, k3, m1r, p1*, repeat from * to * 5 times, m1l, k3, p1, k3, m1r, sm, yo, ssk, k2. (77 sts)

Row 20: K4, sm, p4, *k1, p4* repeat from * to * 12 times, sm, k4.

Row 21: K2, k2tog, yo, sm, *k3, p1, k1, p1, k3, p1*, repeat from * to * 5 times, k3, p1, k1, p1, k3, sm, yo, ssk, k2.

Row 22: K4, sm, p3, k1, p1, k1, p3, *k1, p3, k1, p1, k1, p3*, repeat from * to * 5 times, sm, k4.

Row 23: K2, k2tog, yo, sm, *m1l, k2, p1, k1, p1, k1, p1, k2, m1r, p1*, repeat from * to * 5 times, m1l, k2, p1, k1, p1, k1, p1, k2, m1r, sm, yo, ssk, k2. (91 sts)

Row 24: K4, sm, p3, k1, p1, k1, p1, k1, p3, *k1, p3, k1, p1, k1, p1, k1, p3*, repeat from * to * 5 times, sm, k4.

Row 25: K2, k2tog, yo, sm, *k2, (p1, k1) × 3, p1, k2, p1*, repeat from * to * 5 times, k2, (p1, k1) × 3, p1, k2, sm, yo, ssk, k2.

Row 26: K4, sm, p2, (k1, p1) × 3, k1, p2, *k1, p2, (k1, p1) × 3, k1, p2*, repeat from * to * 5 times, sm, k4.

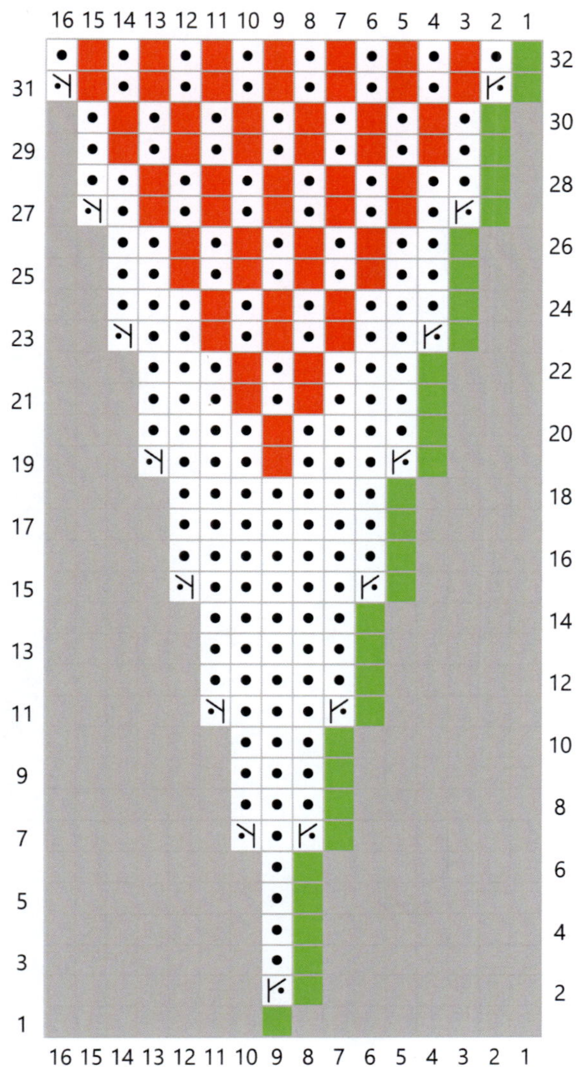

- RS: knit / WS: purl
- RS: m1 right leaning / WS: m1 purlwise right leaning
- RS: m1 left leaning / WS: m1 purlwise left leaning
- RS: purl / WS: knit
- RS: m1 purlwise right leaning, p1 / WS: k1, m1 right leaning
- RS: m1 purlwise left leaning / WS: m1 left leaning
- grey no stitch
- Edge stitch
- knit sts in colour for better visibility

Chart 1. Pyramids of Giza

Row 27: K2, k2tog, yo, sm, *m1l, (k1, p1) × 5, k1, m1r, p1*, repeat from * to * 5 times, m1l, (k1, p1) × 5, k1, m1r, sm, yo, ssk, k2. (105 sts)

Row 28: K4, sm, p2, (k1, p1) × 4, k1, p2, *k1, p2, (k1, p1) × 4, k1, p2*, repeat from * to * 5 times, sm, k4.

Row 29: K2, k2tog, yo, sm, *k1, p1*, repeat from * to * 47 times, k1, sm, yo, ssk, k2.

Row 30: K4, sm, p1, *k1, p1*, repeat from * to * 47 times, sm, k4.

Row 31: K2, k2tog, yo, sm, *m1l, (p1, k1) × 6, p1, m1r, p1*, repeat from * to * 5 times, m1l, (p1, k1) × 6, p1, m1r, sm, yo, ssk, k2. (119 sts)

Row 32: K4, sm, p1, *k1, p1*, repeat from * to * 54 times, sm, k4.

Temple of Artemis

Cables and purls (purls will become drop sts)

If you will be changing colours each section as opposed to working with one colour, or a gradient, then purl rows 33, 35 and 37, to give a smoother transition. When changing colours, use your next colour for row 33 and 34, then the original colour for 35 and 36, then continue in your next colour for 37 onwards.

Row 33 (WS): K2, k2tog, yo, sm, knit to 4 sts before end, sm, yo, ssk, k2.

Row 34 (RS): K4, sm, m1l, *slip last stitch on to left needle knitwise, ktbl the second stitch on the left needle and knit the first stitch*, repeat from * to * until 4 sts before the end, remove marker, slip last st back to the left needle, pm, k2tog, k3.

Row 35: K2, k2tog, yo, sm, *m1l, k15, m1r, k1*, repeat from * to * 5 times, m1l, k15, m1r, sm, yo, ssk, k2. (133 sts)

Row 36: K4, sm, *k2tog, yo*, repeat from * to * until 5 sts before end, k1, sm, k4.

Row 37: K2, k2tog, yo, sm, knit to 4 sts before end, sm, yo, ssk, k2.

Row 38: Repeat row 34.

Row 39: K2, k2tog, yo, sm, *m1l, (p2, p2tog tbl, yo, k1) × 3, p2, m1r, k1*, repeat from * to * 5 times, m1l, (p2, p2tog tbl, yo, k1) × 3, p2, m1r, sm, yo, ssk, k2. (147 sts)

Row 40: K4, sm, p1, (1/1 RC, p3) × 3, 1/1 RC, p1, *p2, (1/1 RC, p3) × 3, 1/1 RC, p1*, repeat from * to * 5 times, sm, k4.

Row 41: K2, k2tog, yo, sm, *k1, (p2, k3) × 3, p2, k2*, repeat from * to * 5 times, K1, (p2, k3) × 3, p2, k1, sm, yo, ssk, k2.

Row 42: K4, sm, p1, (k2, p3) × 3, k2, p1, *p2, (k2, p3) × 3, k2, p1*, repeat from * to * 5 times, sm, k4.

Row 43: K2, k2tog, yo, sm, *m1l, k1, (p2, k3) × 3, p2, k1, m1r, k1*, repeat from * to * 5 times, m1l, k1, (p2, k3) × 3, p2, k1, m1r, sm, yo, ssk, k2. (161 sts)

Row 44: K4, sm, p2, 1/1 RC, (p3, 1/1 RC) × 3, p2, *(p3, 1/1 RC) × 4, p2*, repeat from * to * 5 times, sm, k4.

Row 45: K2, k2tog, yo, sm, *k2, (p2, k3) × 4*, repeat from * to * 5 times, k2, (p2, k3) × 3, p2, k2, sm, yo, ssk, k2.

Row 46: K4, sm, p2, k2, (p3, k2) × 3, p2, *(p3, k2) × 4, p2*, repeat from * to * 5 times, sm, k4.

Row 47: K2, k2tog, yo, sm, *m1l, k2, (p2, k3) × 3, p2, k2, m1r, p1*, repeat from * to * 5 times, m1l, k2, (p2, k3) × 3, p2, k2, m1r, sm, yo, ssk, k2. (175 sts)

Row 48: K4, sm, (p3, 1/1 RC) × 4, p3, *k1, (p3, 1/1 RC) × 4, p3*, repeat from * to * 5 times, sm, k4.

Row 49: K2, k2tog, yo, sm, *(k3, p2) × 4, k3, p1*, repeat from * to * 5 times, (k3, p2) × 4, k3, sm, yo, ssk, k2.

Row 50: K4, sm, (p3, k2) × 4, p3, *k1, (p3, k2) × 4, p3*, repeat from * to * 5 times, sm, k4.

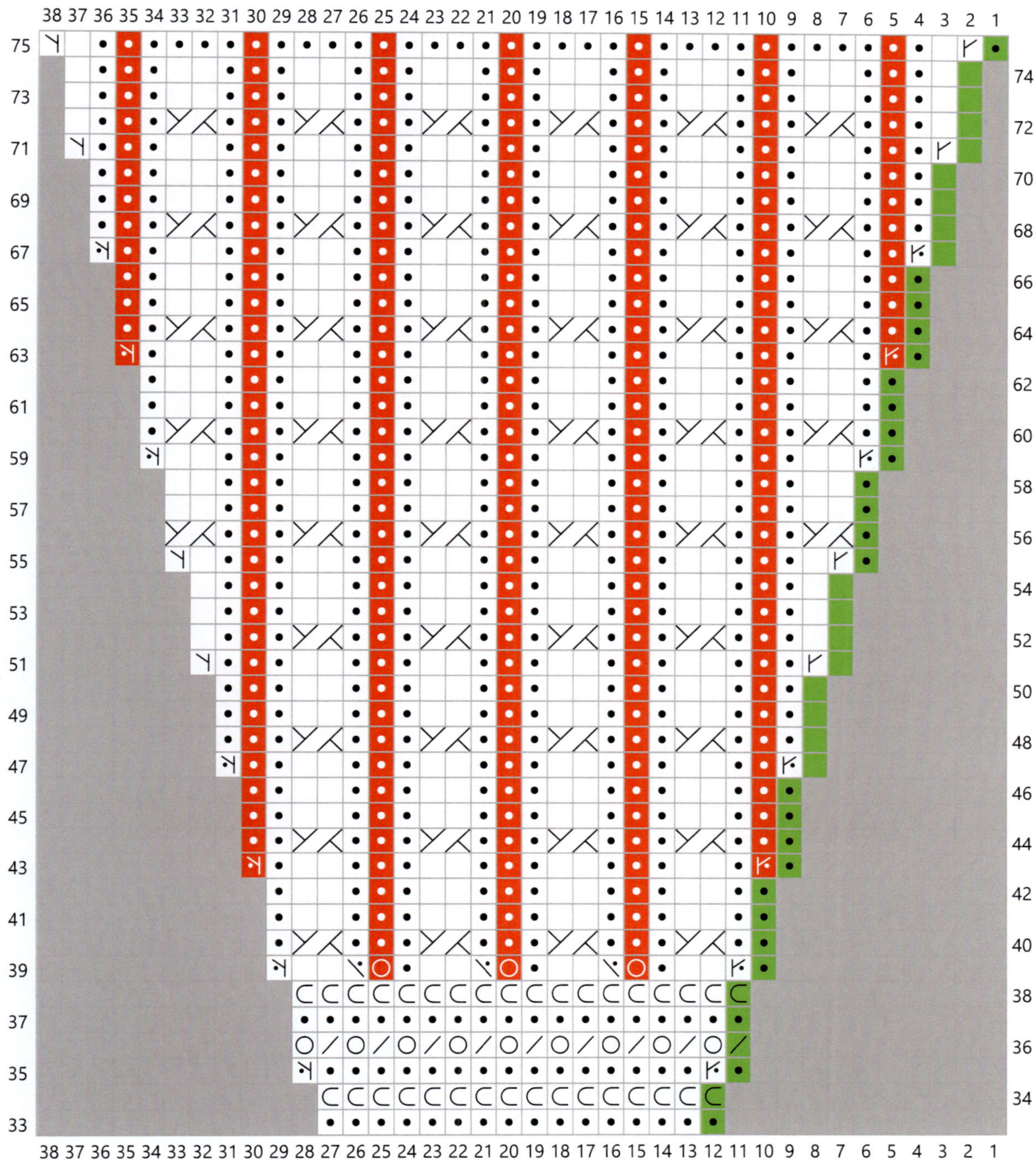

- (blank square) RS: knit / WS: purl
- (dot) RS: purl / WS: knit
- Lateral Braid Stitch
- yo
- RS: m1 right leaning / WS: m1 purlwise right leaning
- RS: m1 left leaning / WS: m1 purlwise left leaning
- RS: m1 purlwise right leaning / WS: m1 right leaning
- RS: m1 purlwise left leaning / WS: m1 left leaning
- RS: k2tog / WS: p2tog
- RS: p2tog tbl / WS: twisted ssk
- 1/1 RC
- Drop these stitches on row 78
- Edge Stitch
- grey no stitch

Chart 2. Temple of Artemis

Row 51: K2, k2tog, yo, sm, *m1pl, (k3, p2) × 4, k3, m1pr, p1*, repeat from * to * 5 times, m1pl, (k3, p2) × 4, k3, m1pr, sm, yo, ssk, k2. (189 sts)

Row 52: K4, sm, k1, (p3, 1/1 RC) × 4, p3, k1, *k2, (p3, 1/1 RC) × 4, p3, k1*, repeat from * to * 5 times, sm, k4.

Row 53: K2, k2tog, yo, sm, *p1, (k3, p2) × 5*, repeat from * to * 5 times, p1, (k3, p2) × 4, k3, p1, sm, yo, ssk, k2.

Row 54: K4, sm, k1, p3, (k2, p3) × 4, k1, *(k2, p3) × 5, k1*, repeat from * to * 5 times, sm, k4.

Row 55: K2, k2tog, yo, sm, *m1pl, p1, (k3, p2) × 4, k3, p1, m1pr, k1*, repeat from * to * 5 times, m1pl, p1, (k3, p2) × 4, k3, p1, m1pr, sm, yo, ssk, k2. (203 sts)

Row 56: K4, sm, (1/1 RC, p3) × 5, 1/1 RC, *p1, (1/1 RC, p3) × 5, 1/1 RC*, repeat from * to * 5 times, sm, k4.

Row 57: K2, k2tog, yo, sm, *(p2, k3) × 5, p2, k1*, repeat from * to * 5 times, (p2, k3) × 5, p2, sm, yo, ssk, k2.

Row 58: K4, sm, (k2, p3) × 5, k2, *p1, (k2, p3) × 5, k2*, repeat from * to * 5 times, sm, k4.

Row 59: K2, k2tog, yo, sm, *m1l, (p2, k3) × 5, p2, m1r, k1*, repeat from * to * 5 times, m1l, (p2, k3) × 5, p2, m1r, sm, yo, ssk, k2. (217 sts)

Row 60: K4, sm, p1, (1/1 RC, p3) × 5, 1/1 RC, p1, *p2, (1/1 RC, p3) × 5, 1/1 RC, p1*, repeat from * to * 5 times, sm, k4.

Row 61: K2, k2tog, yo, sm, *k1, (p2, k3) × 5, p2, k2*, repeat from * to * 5 times, k1, (p2, k3) × 5, p2, k2, sm, yo, ssk, k2.

Row 62: K4, sm, p1, (k2, p3) × 5, k2, p1, *p2, (k2, p3) × 5, k2, p1*, repeat from * to * 5 times, sm, k4.

Row 63: K2, k2tog, yo, sm, *m1l, k1, (p2,

k3) × 5, p2, k1, m1r, k1*, repeat from * to * 5 times, m1l, k1, (p2, k3) × 5, p2, k1, m1r, sm, yo, ssk, k2. (231 sts)

Row 64: K4, sm, p2, 1/1 RC, (p3, 1/1 RC) × 5, p2 *(p3, 1/1 RC) × 6, p2*, repeat from * to * 5 times, sm, k4.

Row 65: K2, k2tog, yo, sm, *k2, (p2, k3) × 6*, repeat from * to * 5 times, k2, (p2, k3) × 5, p2, k2, sm, yo, ssk, k2.

Row 66: K4, sm, p2, k2, (p3, k2) × 5, p2, *(p3, k2) × 6, p2*, repeat from * to * 5 times, sm, k4.

Row 67: K2, k2tog, yo, sm, *m1l, k2, (p2, k3) × 5, p2, k2, m1r, p1*, repeat from * to * 5 times, m1l, k2, (p2, k3) × 5, p2, k2, m1r, sm, yo, ssk, k2. (245 sts)

Row 68: K4, sm, (p3, 1/1 RC) × 6, p3, *k1, (p3, 1/1 RC) × 6, p3*, repeat from * to * 5 times, sm, k4.

Row 69: K2, k2tog, yo, sm, *(k3, p2) × 6, k3, p1*, repeat from * to * 5 times, (k3, p2) × 6, k3, sm, yo, ssk, k2.

Row 70: K4, sm, (p3, k2) × 6, p3, *k1, (p3, k2) × 6, p3*, repeat from * to * 5 times, sm, k4.

Row 71: K2, k2tog, yo, sm, *m1pl, (k3, p2) × 6, k3, m1pr, p1*, repeat from * to * 5 times, m1pl, (k3, p2) × 6, k3, m1pr, sm, yo, ssk, k2. (259 sts)

Row 72: K4, sm, k1, (p3, 1/1 RC) × 6, p3, k1, *k2, (p3, 1/1 RC) × 6, p3, k1*, repeat from * to * 5 times, sm, k4.

Row 73: K2, k2tog, yo, sm, *p1, (k3, p2) × 7*, repeat from * to * 5 times, p1, (k3, p2) × 6, k3, p1, sm, yo, ssk, k2.

Row 74: K4, sm, k1, p3, (k2, p3) × 6, k1, *(k2, p3) × 7, k1*, repeat from * to * 5 times, sm, k4.

Row 75: K2, k2tog, yo, sm, *m1pl, p1, k33, p1, m1pr, k1*, repeat from * to * 5 times, m1pl, p1, k33, p1, m1pr, sm, yo, ssk, k2. (273 sts)

Hanging Gardens of Babylon

Lace

Row 76: K4, sm, 1/1 RC, p2, (k4, p1) × 5, k4, p2, 1/1 RC, *p1, 1/1 RC, p2, (k4, p1) × 5, k4, p2, 1/1 RC*, repeat from * to * 5 times, sm, k4.

Row 77: K2, k2tog, yo, sm, *p2, k33, p2, k1*, repeat from * to * 5 times, p2, k33, p2, sm, yo, ssk, k2.

Row 78: K4, sm, k2, p1, DnSK, k2, (k2tog, DnSKPK, ssk, k2, DnSK, k2) × 2, k2tog, DnSKPK, ssk, k2, DnSK, p1, k2, *k3, p1, DnSK, k2, (k2tog, DnSKPK, ssk, k2, DnSK, k2) × 2, k2tog, DnSKPK, ssk, k2, DnSK, p1, k2*, repeat from * to * 5 times, sm, k4.

Row 79: K2, k2tog, yo, sm, *m1l, p2, k1, p31, k1, p2, m1r, p1*, repeat from * to * 5 times, m1l, p2, k1, p31, k1, p2, m1r, sm, yo, ssk, k2. (287 sts)

Row 80: K4, sm, p1, 1/1 RC, p1, (k1, k2tog, yo, k5, yo, ssk) × 3, k1, p1, 1/1 RC, p1, *k1, p1, 1/1 RC, p1, (k1, k2tog, yo, k5, yo, ssk) × 3, k1, p1, 1/1 RC, p1*, repeat from * to * 5 times, sm, k4.

Row 81: K2, k2tog, yo, sm, *k1, p2, k1, p31, k1, p2, k1, p1*, repeat from * to * 5 times, k1, p2, k1, p31, k1, p2, k1, sm, yo, ssk, k2.

Row 82: K4, sm, p1, k2, p1, k2tog, (yo, k2tog, yo, k3, yo, ssk, yo, cdd) × 2, yo, k2tog, yo, k3, (yo, ssk) × 2, p1, k2, p1, *k1, p1, k2, p1, k2tog, (yo, k2tog, yo, k3, yo, ssk, yo, cdd) × 2, yo, k2tog, yo, k3, (yo, ssk) × 2, p1, k2, p1*, repeat from * to * 5 times, sm, k4.

Row 83: K2, k2tog, yo, sm, *m1pl, k1, p2, k1, p31, k1, p2, k1, m1pr, p1*, repeat from * to * 5 times, m1pl, k1, p2, k1, p31, k1, p2, k1, m1pr, sm, yo, ssk, k2. (301 sts)

Row 84: K4, sm, k1, p1, 1/1 RC, p1, (k1, (yo, ssk) × 2, k1, (k2tog, yo) × 2) × 3, k1, p1, 1/1 RC, p1, k1, *k2, p1, 1/1 RC, p1, (k1, (yo, ssk) × 2, k1, (k2tog, yo) × 2) × 3, k1, p1, 1/1 RC, p1, k1*, repeat from * to * 5 times, sm, k4.

Row 85: K2, k2tog, yo, sm, *p1, k1, p2, k1, p31, (k1, p2) × 2*, repeat from * to * 5 times, p1, k1, p2, k1, p31, k1, p2, k1, p1, sm, yo, ssk, k2.

Row 86: K4, sm, k1, p1, k2, p1, (k1, yo, ssk, k2tog, yo) × 6, k1, p1, k2, p1, k1, *(k2, p1) × 2, (k1, yo, ssk, k2tog, yo) × 6, k1, p1, k2, p1, k1*, repeat from * to * 5 times, sm, k4.

Row 87: K2, k2tog, yo, sm, *m1pl, p1, k1, p2, k1, p31, k1, p2, k1, p1, m1pr, p1*, repeat from * to * 5 times, m1pl, p1, k1, p2, k1, p31, k1, p2, k1, p1, m1pr, sm, yo, ssk, k2. (315 sts)

Row 88: K4, sm, k2, p1, 1/1 RC, p1, (k1, (yo, ssk) × 2, k1, (k2tog, yo) × 2) × 3, k1, p1, 1/1 RC, p1, k2, *k3, p1, 1/1 RC, p1, (k1, (yo, ssk) × 2, k1, (k2tog, yo) × 2) × 3, k1, p1, 1/1 RC, p1, k2*, repeat from * to * 5 times, sm, k4.

Row 89: K2, k2tog, yo, sm, purl to 4 sts before end, sm, yo, ssk, k2.

Row 90: K4, sm, k4, k2tog, yo, kfb, (yo, ssk × 2, k1, k2tog × 2, yo, kyok) × 2, yo, ssk × 2, k1, k2tog × 2, yo, kfb, yo, ssk, k4, *k5, k2tog, yo, kfb, (yo, ssk × 2, k1, k2tog × 2, yo, kyok) × 2, yo, ssk × 2, k1, k2tog × 2, yo, kfb, yo, ssk, k4*, repeat from * to * 5 times, sm, k4.

Row 91: K2, k2tog, yo, sm, *m1pl, p43, m1pr, p1*, repeat from * to * 5 times, m1pl, p43, m1pr, sm, yo, ssk, k2. (329 sts)

Row 92: K4, sm, k3, yo, k2tog × 2, yo, k1, m1, (ssk, yo, ssk, k1, (k2tog, yo) × 2, k1, yo) × 2, ssk, yo, ssk, k1, k2tog, yo, k2tog, m1, k1, yo, ssk × 2, yo, k3, *k4, yo, k2tog × 2, yo, k1, m1, (ssk, yo, ssk, k1, (k2tog, yo) × 2, k1, yo) × 2, ssk, yo, ssk, k1, k2tog, yo, k2tog, m1, k1, yo, ssk × 2, yo, k3*, repeat from * to * 5 times, sm, k4.

Row 93: K2, k2tog, yo, sm, purl to 4 sts before end, sm, yo, ssk, k2.

Row 94: K4, sm, k2, m1r, k2, (yo, k2tog) × 2, yo, k1, (yo, ssk, yo, cdd, yo, k2tog, yo, cdd) × 2, yo, ssk, yo, cdd, yo, k2tog, yo, k1, (yo, ssk) × 2, yo, k2, m1l, k2, *k3, m1r, k2, (yo, k2tog) × 2, yo, k1, (yo, ssk, yo, cdd, yo, k2tog, yo, cdd) × 2, yo, ssk, yo, cdd, yo, k2tog, yo, k1, (yo, ssk) × 2, yo, k2, m1l, k2*, repeat from * to * 5 times, sm, k4.

Row 95: K2, k2tog, yo, sm, *m1pl, p45, m1pr, p1*, repeat from * to * 5 times, m1pl, p45, m1pr, sm, yo, ssk, k2. (343 sts)

Row 96: K4, sm, (k2tog, yo) × 2, k2tog, (k1, yo) × 2, k2tog, yo, cdd, yo, ssk, yo, k2, yo, ssk, k1, k2tog, yo, k3, yo, ssk, k1, k2tog, yo, k2, yo, k2tog, yo, cdd, yo, ssk, (yo, k1) × 2, (ssk, yo) × 2, ssk, *k1, (k2tog, yo) × 2, k2tog, (k1, yo) × 2, k2tog, yo, cdd, yo, ssk, yo, k2, yo, ssk, k1, k2tog, yo, k3, yo, ssk, k1, k2tog, yo, k2, yo, k2tog, yo, cdd, yo, ssk, (yo, k1) × 2, (ssk, yo) × 2, ssk*, repeat from * to * 5 times, sm, k4.

Row 97: K2, k2tog, yo, sm, *p4, ssp, yo, pyopcdd, yo, p2tog, p1, ssp, yo, (pyopcdd, sl wyif, yo, cddp, yo, sl wyif) × 2, pyopcdd, yo, p2tog, p1, ssp, yo, pyopcdd, yo, p2tog, p5*, repeat from * to * 5 times, p4, ssp, yo, pyopcdd, yo, p2tog, p1, ssp, yo, (pyopcdd, sl wyif, yo, cddp, yo, sl wyif) × 2, pyopcdd, yo, p2tog, p1, ssp, yo, pyopcdd, yo, p2tog, p4, sm, yo, ssk, k2.

Row 98: K4, sm, k1, k2tog, yo, k2tog, (yo, k2tog, yo, k1, yo, ssk, yo, cdd) × 4, yo, k2tog, yo, k1, (yo, ssk) × 3, k1, *k2, k2tog, yo, k2tog, (yo, k2tog, yo, k1, yo, ssk, yo, cdd) × 4, yo, k2tog, yo, k1, (yo, ssk) × 3, k1*, repeat from * to * 5 times, sm, k4.

Row 99: K2, k2tog, yo, sm, *m1pl, p47, m1pr, p1*, repeat from * to * 5 times, m1pl, p47, m1pr, sm, yo, ssk, k2. (357 sts)

Row 100: K4, sm, k1, (yo, k2tog) × 2, (yo, k2tog, yo, cdd, yo, ssk, yo, k1) × 4, yo, k2tog, yo, cdd, (yo, ssk) × 3, yo, k1, *k2, (yo, k2tog) × 2, (yo, k2tog, yo, cdd, yo, ssk, yo, k1) × 4, yo, k2tog, yo, cdd, (yo, ssk) × 3, yo, k1*, repeat from * to * 5 times, sm, k4.

Row 101: K2, k2tog, yo, sm, purl to 4 sts before end, sm, yo, ssk, k2.

Row 102: K4, sm, k1, (k2tog, yo, kyokcdd, yo, ssk, k1) × 6, *k2, (k2tog, yo, kyokcdd, yo, ssk, k1) × 6*, repeat from * to * 5 times, sm, k4.

Row 103: K2, k2tog, yo, sm, *m1pl, ssp, (yo, ssp, yo, p1, yo, p2tog, yo, cddp) × 5, yo, ssp, yo, p1, (yo, p2tog) × 2, m1pr, p1*, repeat from * to * 5 times, m1pl, ssp, (yo, ssp, yo, p1, yo, p2tog, yo, cddp) × 5, yo, ssp, yo, p1, (yo, p2tog) × 2, m1pr, sm, yo, ssk, k2. (371 sts)

Row 104: K4, sm, knit to 4 sts before end, sm, k4.

Row 105: K2, k2tog, yo, sm, *yo, ssp, (yo, ssp, yo, cddp, yo, p2tog, yo, p1) × 5, yo, ssp, yo, cddp, (yo, p2tog) × 2, yo, p1*, repeat from * to * 5 times, yo, ssp, (yo, ssp, yo, cddp, yo, p2tog, yo, p1) × 5, yo, ssp, yo, cddp, (yo, p2tog) × 2, yo, sm, yo, ssk, k2.

Row 106: K4, sm, knit to 4 sts before end, sm, k4.

Row 107: K2, k2tog, yo, sm, *m1pl, p1, yo, ssp, (yo, p2tog, p1, ssp, yo, pyopcdd) × 5, yo, p2tog, p1, ssp, yo, p2tog, yo, p1, m1pr, p1*, repeat from * to * 5 times, m1pl, p1, yo, ssp, (yo, p2tog, p1, ssp, yo, pyopcdd) × 5, yo, p2tog, p1, ssp, yo, p2tog, yo, p1, m1pr, sm, yo, ssk, k2. (385 sts)

RS: knit
WS: purl

RS: purl
WS: knit

yo

RS: m1
WS: m1 purlwise

RS: m1 purlwise left leaning
WS: m1 left leaning

RS: m1 purlwise right leaning
WS: m1 right leaning

RS: m1 left leaning
WS: m1 purlwise left leaning

RS: m1 right leaning
WS: m1 purlwise right leaning

RS: knit into fb
WS: purl into fb

RS: (k1, p1, k1) in 1 stitch
WS: (p1, k1, p1) in 1 stitch

RS: (k1, yo, k1) in 1 stitch
WS: (p1, yo, p1) in 1 stitch

RS: (p1, yo, p1) in 1 stitch
WS: (k1, yo, k1) in 1 stitch

RS: (k1, yo, k1) in cdd sts
WS: (p1, yo, p1) in cdd sts

RS: k2tog
WS: p2tog

RS: ssk
WS: ssp

RS: p2tog tbl
WS: twisted ssk

RS: central double decrease
WS: central double decrease purl

RS: slip
WS: slip purlwise with yarn in front

1/1 RC

grey no stitch

Drop these stitches on row 78 and knit into the bar

Edge stitch

DnSK or DnSKPK: Drop the stitch below and knit into the bar

Key for Chart 3. Hanging Gardens of Babylon (next page)

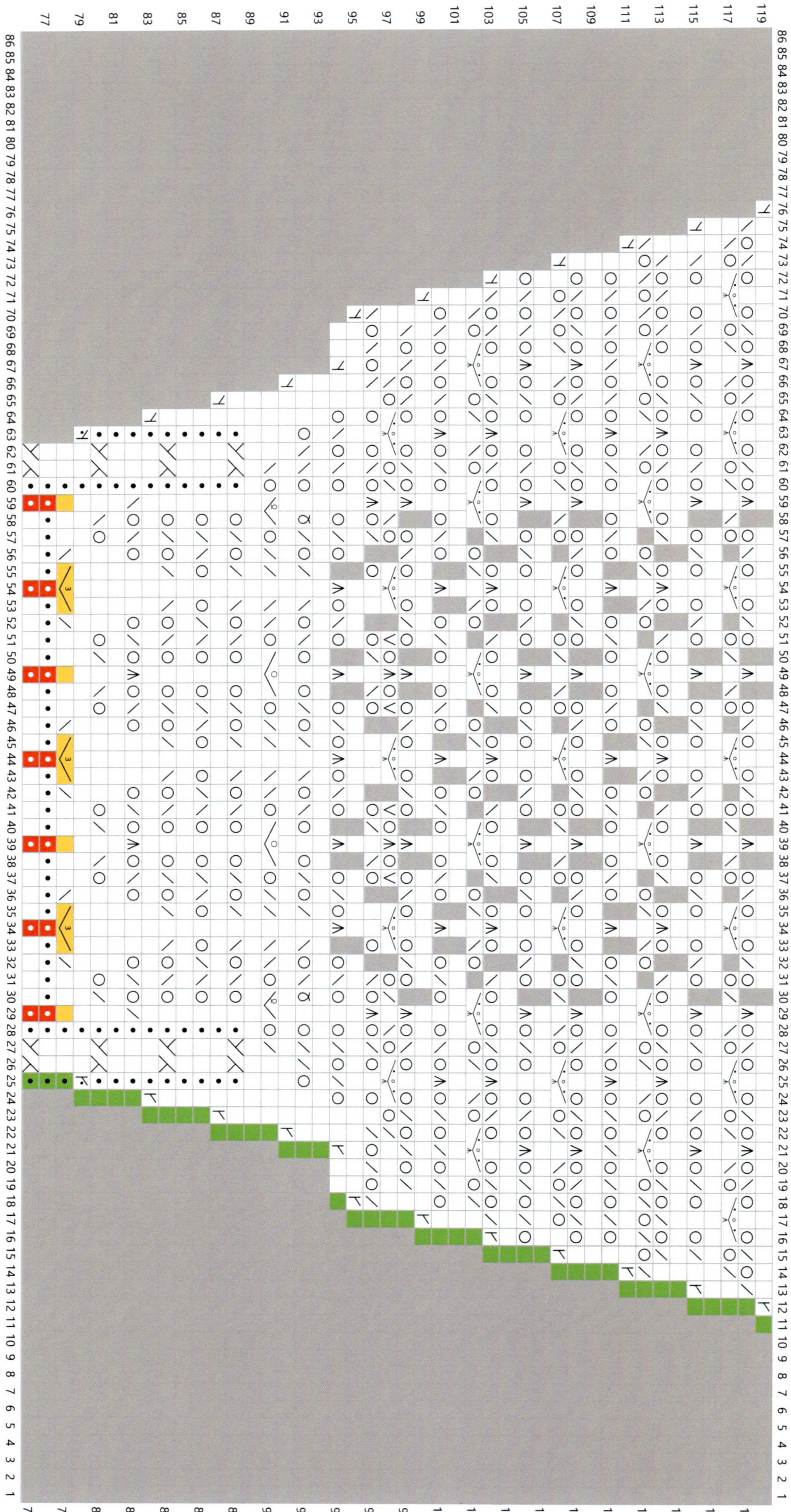

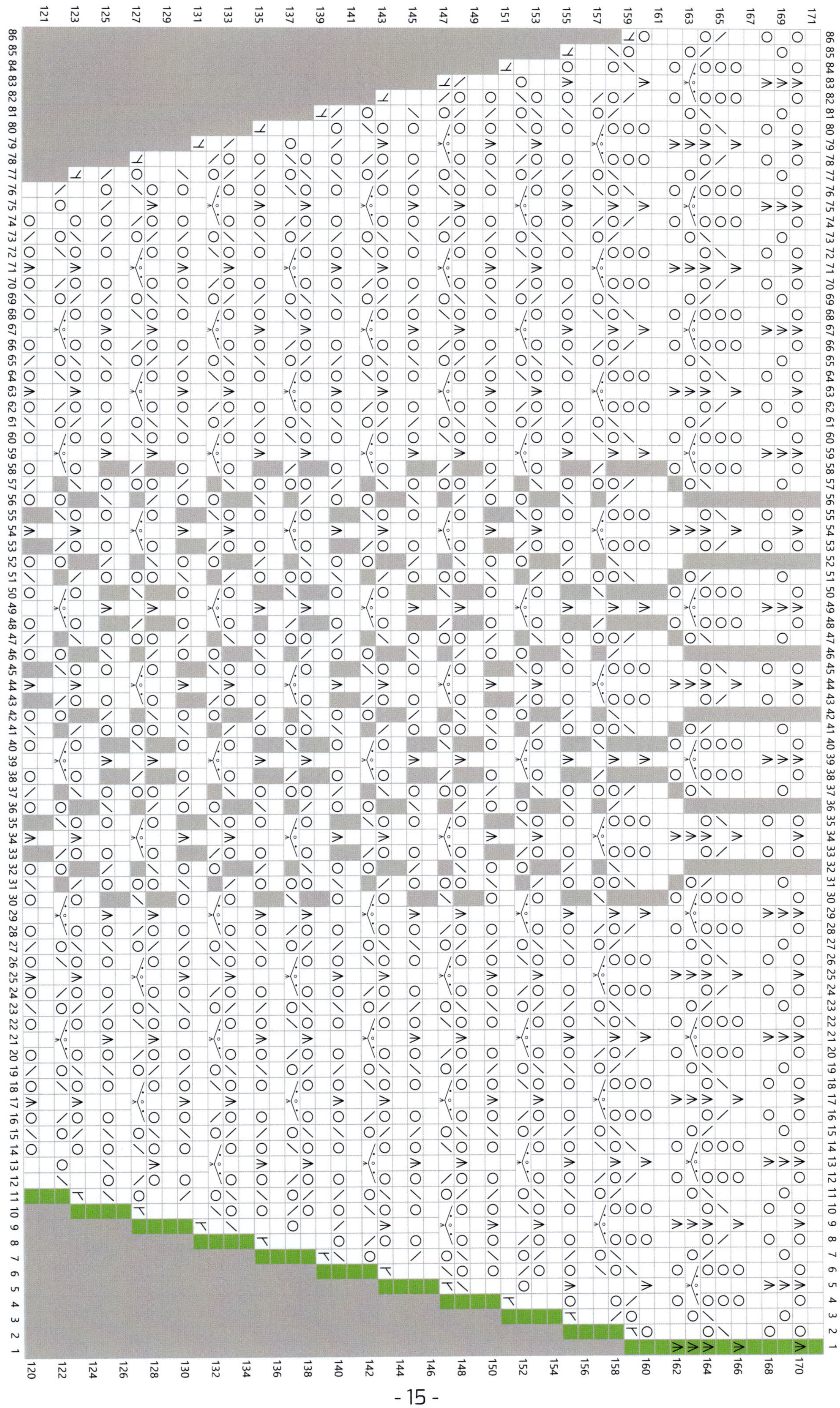

Row 108: K4, sm, k2, yo, k2tog, (yo, ssk, yo, cdd, yo, k2tog, yo, k1) × 5, yo, ssk, yo, cdd, yo, k2tog, yo, ssk, yo, k1, *k2, yo, k2tog, (yo, ssk, yo, cdd, yo, k2tog, yo, k1) × 5, yo, ssk, yo, cdd, yo, k2tog, yo, ssk, yo, k1*, repeat from * to * 5 times, sm, k4.

Row 109: K2, k2tog, yo, sm, purl to 4 sts before end, sm, yo, ssk, k2.

Row 110: K4, sm, k1, (yo, k2tog) × 2, yo, k2tog, (yo, k2tog, yo, cdd, yo, ssk, yo, k1) × 4, yo, k2tog, yo, cdd, (yo, ssk) × 4, yo, k1, *k2, (yo, k2tog) × 2, yo, k2tog, (yo, k2tog, yo, cdd, yo, ssk, yo, k1) × 4, yo, k2tog, yo, cdd, (yo, ssk) × 4, yo, k1*, repeat from * to * 5 times, sm, k4.

Row 111: K2, k2tog, yo, sm, *m1pl, p53, m1pr, p1*, repeat from * to * 5 times, m1pl, p53, m1pr, sm, yo, ssk, k2. (399 sts)

Row 112: K4, sm, (k2tog, yo) × 2, (k2tog, yo, kyokcdd, yo, ssk, k1) × 5, k2tog, yo, kyokcdd, (yo, ssk) × 2, yo, ssk, *k1, (k2tog, yo) × 2, (k2tog, yo, kyokcdd, yo, ssk, k1) × 5, k2tog, yo, kyokcdd, (yo, ssk) × 2, yo, ssk*, repeat from * to * 5 times, sm, k4.

Row 113: K2, k2tog, yo, sm, *p1, ssp, yo, ssp, (yo, ssp, yo, p1, yo, p2tog, yo, cddp) × 5, yo, ssp, yo, p1, (yo, p2tog) × 3, p2*, repeat from * to * 5 times, p1, ssp, yo, ssp, (yo, ssp, yo, p1, yo, p2tog, yo, cddp) × 5, yo, ssp, yo, p1, (yo, p2tog) × 3, p1, sm, yo, ssk, k2.

Row 114: K4, sm, knit to 4 sts before end, sm, k4.

Row 115: K2, k2tog, yo, sm, *m1pl, p1, ssp, (yo, p1, yo, ssp, yo, cddp, yo, p2tog) × 6, yo, p1, yo, p2tog, p1, m1pr, p1*, repeat from * to * 5 times, m1pl, p1, ssp, (yo, p1, yo, ssp, yo, cddp, yo, p2tog) × 6, yo, p1, yo, p2tog, p1, m1pr, sm, yo, ssk, k2. (413 sts)

Row 116: K4, sm, knit to 4 sts before end, sm, k4.

Row 117: K2, k2tog, yo, sm, *(p1, ssp, yo, pyopcdd, yo, p2tog) × 7, p2*, repeat from * to * 5 times, (p1, ssp, yo, pyopcdd, yo, p2tog) × 7, p1, sm, yo, ssk, k2.

Row 118: K4, sm, k2tog, (yo, k2tog, yo, k1, yo, ssk, yo, cdd) × 6, yo, k2tog, yo, k1, (yo, ssk) × 2, *k1, k2tog, (yo, k2tog, yo, k1, yo, ssk, yo, cdd) × 6, yo, k2tog, yo, k1, (yo, ssk) × 2* repeat from * to * 5 times, sm, k4.

Row 119: K2, k2tog, yo, sm, *m1pl, p57, m1pr, p1*, repeat from * to * 5 times, m1pl, p57, m1pr, sm, yo, ssk, k2. (427 sts)

Row 120: K4, sm, k3, (yo, k2tog, yo, cdd, yo, ssk, yo, k1) × 6, yo, k2tog, yo, cdd, yo, ssk, yo, k2, *k3, (yo, k2tog, yo, cdd, yo, ssk, yo, k1) × 6, yo, k2tog, yo, cdd, yo, ssk, yo, k2*, repeat from * to * 5 times, sm, k4.

Row 121: K2, k2tog, yo, sm, purl to 4 sts before end, sm, yo, ssk, k2.

Row 122: K4, sm, k2tog, yo, k1, (yo, ssk, k1, k2tog, yo, kyokcdd) × 6, yo, ssk, k1, k2tog, yo, k1, yo, ssk, *k1, k2tog, yo, k1, (yo, ssk, k1, k2tog, yo, kyokcdd) × 6, yo, ssk, k1, k2tog, yo, k1, yo, ssk*, repeat from * to * 5 times, sm, k4.

Row 123: K2, k2tog, yo, sm, *m1pl, p2, (yo, p2tog, yo, cddp, yo, ssp, yo, p1) × 6, yo, p2tog, yo, cddp, yo, ssp, yo, p2, m1pr, p1*, repeat from * to * 5 times, m1pl, p2, (yo, p2tog, yo, cddp, yo, ssp, yo, p1) × 6, yo, p2tog, yo, cddp, yo, ssp, yo, p2, m1pr, sm, yo, k2tog, k2. (441 sts)

Row 124: K4, sm, knit to 4 sts before end, sm, k4.

Row 125: K2, k2tog, yo, sm, *(ssp, yo) × 2, ssp, (yo, p1, yo, ssp, yo, cddp, yo, p2tog) × 6, yo, p1, (yo, p2tog) × 3, p1*, repeat from * to * 5 times, (ssp, yo) × 2, ssp, (yo, p1, yo, ssp, yo, cddp, yo, p2tog) × 6, yo, p1, (yo, p2tog) × 3, sm, yo, k2tog, k2.

Row 126: K4, sm, knit to 4 sts before end, sm, k4.

Row 127: K2, k2tog, yo, sm, *m1pl, (yo, p2tog, p1, ssp, yo, pypcdd) × 7, yo, p2tog, p1, ssp, yo, m1pr, p1*, repeat from * to * 5 times, m1pl, (yo, p2tog, p1, ssp, yo, pypcdd) × 7, yo, p2tog, p1, ssp, yo, m1pr, sm, yo, k2tog, k2. (455 sts)

Row 128: K4, sm, k2, (yo, cdd, yo, k2tog, yo, k1, yo, ssk) × 7, yo, cdd, yo, k2, *k3, (yo, cdd, yo, k2tog, yo, k1, yo, ssk) × 7, yo, cdd, yo, k2*, repeat from * to * 5 times, sm, k4.

Row 129: K2, k2tog, yo, sm, purl to 4 sts before end, sm, yo, ssk, k2.

Row 130: K4, sm, k1, (ssk, yo, k1, yo, k2tog, yo, cdd, yo) × 7, ssk, yo, k1, yo, k2tog, k1, *k2, (ssk, yo, k1, yo, k2tog, yo, cdd, yo) × 7, ssk, yo, k1, yo, k2tog, k1*, repeat from * to * 5 times, sm, k4.

Row 131: K2, k2tog, yo, sm, *m1pl, p63, m1pr, p1*, repeat from * to * 5 times, m1pl, p63, m1pr, sm, yo, k2tog, k2. (469 sts)

Row 132: K4, sm, k2, (k2tog, yo, kyokcdd, yo, ssk, k1) × 8, *k2, (k2tog, yo, kyokcdd, yo, ssk, k1) × 8*, repeat from * to * 5 times, sm, k4.

Row 133: K2, k2tog, yo, sm, *ssp, (yo, ssp, yo, p1, yo, p2tog, yo, cddp) × 7, yo, ssp, yo, p1, (yo, p2tog) × 2, p1*, repeat from * to * 5 times, ssp, (yo, ssp, yo, p1, yo, p2tog, yo, cddp) × 7, yo, ssp, yo, p1, (yo, p2tog) × 2, sm, yo, k2tog, k2.

Row 134: K4, sm, knit to 4 sts before end, sm, k4.

Row 135: K2, k2tog, yo, sm, *m1pl, (p1, yo, ssp, yo, cddp, yo, p2tog, yo) × 8, p1, m1pr, p1*, repeat from * to * 5 times, m1pl, (p1, yo, ssp, yo, cddp, yo, p2tog, yo) × 8, p1, m1pr, sm, yo, k2tog, k2. (483 sts)

Row 136: K4, sm, knit to 4 sts before end, sm, k4.

Row 137: K2, k2tog, yo, sm, *p1, yo, p2tog, (yo, p2tog, p1, ssp, yo, pyopcdd) × 7, yo, p2tog, p1, (ssp, yo) × 2, p2*, repeat from * to * 5 times, p1, yo, p2tog, (yo, p2tog, p1, ssp, yo, pyopcdd) × 7, yo, p2tog, p1, (ssp, yo) × 2, p1 sm, yo, k2tog, k2.

Row 138: K4, sm, k2, (yo, ssk, yo, cdd, yo, k2tog, yo, k1) × 7, yo, ssk, yo, cdd, yo, k2tog, yo, k2, *k3, (yo, ssk, yo, cdd, yo, k2tog, yo, k1) × 7, yo, ssk, yo, cdd, yo, k2tog, yo, k2*, repeat from * to * 5 times, sm, k4.

Row 139: K2, k2tog, yo, sm, *m1pl, p67, m1pr, p1*, repeat from * to * 5 times, m1pl, p67, m1pr, sm, yo, k2tog, k2. (497 sts)

Row 140: K4, sm, k2tog, yo, ssk, (yo, ssk, yo, k1, yo, k2tog, yo, cdd) × 7, yo, ssk, yo, k1, yo, k2tog, (yo, ssk) × 2, *k1, k2tog, yo, ssk, (yo, ssk, yo, k1, yo, k2tog, yo, cdd) × 7, yo, ssk, yo, k1, yo, k2tog, (yo, ssk) × 2*, repeat from * to * 5 times, sm, k4.

Row 141: K2, k2tog, yo, sm, purl to 4 sts before end, sm, yo, ssk, k2.

Row 142: K4, sm, (yo, ssk, k1, k2tog, yo, kyokcdd) × 8, yo, ssk, k1, k2tog, yo, *k1, (yo, ssk, k1, k2tog, yo, kyokcdd) × 8, yo, ssk, k1, k2tog, yo*, repeat from * to * 5 times, sm, k4.

Row 143: K2, k2tog, yo, sm, *m1pl, p1, (yo, cddp, yo, ssp, yo, p1, yo, p2tog) × 8, yo, cddp, yo, p1, m1pr, p1*, repeat from * to * 5 times, m1pl, p1, (yo, cddp, yo, ssp, yo, p1, yo, p2tog) × 8, yo, cddp, yo, p1, m1pr, sm, yo, k2tog, k2. (511 sts)

Row 144: K4, sm, knit to 4 sts before end, sm, k4.

Row 145: K2, k2tog, yo, sm, *p1, (p2tog, yo, p1, yo, ssp, yo, cddp, yo) × 8, p2tog, yo, p1, yo, ssp, p2*, repeat from * to * 5 times, p1, (p2tog, yo, p1, yo, ssp, yo, cddp, yo) × 8, p2tog, yo, p1, yo, ssp, p1, sm, yo, k2tog, k2.

Row 146: K4, sm, knit to 4 sts before end, sm, k4.

Row 147: K2, k2tog, yo, sm, *m1pl, (ssp, yo, pyopcdd, yo, p2tog, p1) × 8, ssp, yo, pyopcdd, yo, p2tog, m1pr, p1*, repeat from * to * 5 times, m1pl, (ssp, yo, pyopcdd, yo, p2tog, p1) × 8, ssp, yo, pyopcdd, yo, p2tog, m1pr, sm, yo, k2tog, k2. (525 sts)

Row 148: K4, sm, k2tog, (yo, k2tog, yo, k1, yo, ssk, yo, cdd) × 8, yo, k2tog, yo, k1, (yo, ssk) × 2, *k1, k2tog, (yo, k2tog, yo, k1, yo, ssk, yo, cdd) × 8, yo, k2tog, yo, k1, (yo, ssk) × 2*, repeat from * to * 5 times, sm, k4.

Row 149: K2, k2tog, yo, sm, purl to 4 sts before end, sm, yo, ssk, k2.

Row 150: K4, sm, k1, (yo, k2tog, yo, cdd, yo, ssk, yo, k1) × 9, *k2, (yo, k2tog, yo, cdd, yo, ssk, yo, k1) × 9*, repeat from * to * 5 times, sm, k4.

Row 151: K2, k2tog, yo, sm, *m1pl, p73, m1pr, p1*, repeat from * to * 5 times, m1pl, p73, m1pr, sm, yo, k2tog, k2. (539 sts)

Row 152: K4, sm, k1, yo, ssk, (yo, ssk, k1, k2tog, yo, kyokcdd) × 8, yo, ssk, k1, (k2tog, yo) × 2, k1, *k2, yo, ssk, (yo, ssk, k1, k2tog, yo, kyokcdd) × 8, yo, ssk, k1, (k2tog, yo) × 2, k1*, repeat from * to * 5 times, sm, k4.

Row 153: K2, k2tog, yo, sm, *p2, (yo, p2tog, yo, cddp, yo, ssp, yo, p1) × 8, yo, p2tog, yo, cddp, yo, ssp, yo, p3*, repeat from * to * 5 times, p2, (yo, p2tog, yo, cddp, yo, ssp, yo, p1) × 8, yo, p2tog, yo, cddp, yo, ssp, yo, p2 sm, yo, k2tog, k2.

Row 154: K4, sm, knit to 4 sts before end, sm, k4.

Row 155: K2, k2tog, yo, sm, *m1pl, (yo, cddp, yo, p2tog, yo, p1, yo, ssp) × 9, yo, cddp, yo, m1pr, p1*, repeat from * to * 5 times, m1pl, (yo, cddp, yo, p2tog, yo, p1, yo, ssp) × 9, yo, cddp, yo, m1pr, sm, yo, k2tog, k2. (553 sts)

Row 156: K4, sm, knit to 4 sts before end, sm, k4.

Row 157: K2, k2tog, yo, sm, *p3, (ssp, yo, pyopcdd, yo, p2tog, p1) × 8, ssp, yo, pyopcdd, yo, p2tog, p4*, repeat from * to * 5 times, p3, (ssp, yo, pyopcdd, yo, p2tog, p1) × 8, ssp, yo, pyopcdd, yo, p2tog, p3, sm, yo, k2tog, k2.

Row 158: K4, sm, ssk, yo, ssk, (yo, k2tog, yo, k1, yo, ssk, yo, cdd) × 8, yo, k2tog, yo, k1, yo, ssk, (yo, k2tog) × 2, *k1, ssk, yo, ssk, (yo, k2tog, yo, k1, yo, ssk, yo, cdd) × 8, yo, k2tog, yo, k1, yo, ssk, (yo, k2tog) × 2*, repeat from * to * 5 times, sm, k4.

Row 159: K2, k2tog, yo, sm, *m1pl, yo, (p2tog, p1, ssp, (p1, yo) × 2, p1) × 9, p2tog, p1, ssp, yo, m1pr, p1*, repeat from * to * 5 times, m1pl, yo, (p2tog, p1, ssp, (p1, yo) × 2, p1) × 9,

p2tog, p1, ssp, yo, m1pr, sm, yo, k2tog, k2. (567 sts)

Row 160: K4, sm, yo, k2, cdd, k2, yo, (k1, yo, k2, cdd, k2, yo) × 9, *(k1, yo, k2, cdd, k2, yo) × 10*, repeat from * to * 5 times, sm, k4.

Row 161: K2, k2tog, yo, sm, purl to 4 sts before end, sm, yo, ssk, k2.

Row 162: K4, sm, k2tog, (k1, yo) × 2, k2, *(cdd, k2, yo, k1, yo, k2) × 9, *(cdd, k2, yo, k1, yo, k2) × 10*, repeat from * to * 4 times, (cdd, k2, yo, k1, yo, k2) × 9, cdd, k2, (yo, k1) × 2, k2tog, sm, k4.

Row 163: K2, k2tog, yo, sm, p2tog, yo, pyopcdd, yo, p1, cddp, (p1, yo, pyopcdd, yo, p1, cddp) × 9, *(p1, yo, pyopcdd, yo, p1, cddp) × 10*, repeat from * to * 4 times, (p1, yo, pyopcdd, yo, p1, cddp) × 9, p1, yo, pyopcdd, yo, p2tog, sm, yo, k2tog, k2.

Row 164: K4, sm, k1, yo, k2tog, yo, k1, yo, ssk, yo, (cdd, yo, k2tog, yo, k1, yo, ssk, yo) × 9, *(cdd, yo, k2tog, yo, k1, yo, ssk, yo) × 10*, repeat from * to * 5 times, k1, sm, k4. (569 sts)

Row 165: K2, k2tog, yo, sm, k1, *(ssp, (p1, yo) × 2, p1, p2tog, p1) × 10*, repeat from * to * 6 times, k1, sm, yo, k2tog, k2.

Row 166: K4, sm, k2tog, k2, yo, k1, yo, k2, (cdd, k2, yo, k1, yo, k2) × 9, *(cdd, k2, yo, k1, yo, k2) × 10*, repeat from * to * 5 times, (cdd, k2, yo, k1, yo, k2) × 9, cdd, k2, (yo, k1) × 2, cdd, sm, k4. (568 sts)

Row 167: K2, k2tog, yo, sm, purl to 4 sts before end, sm, yo, ssk, k2.

Row 168: K4, sm, *(k1, yo, k2, cdd, k2, yo) × 10*, repeat from * to * 6 times, sm, k4.

Row 169: K2, k2tog, yo, sm, *p1, (yo, p1, cddp, p1, yo, p3) × 9, yo, p1, cddp, p1, yo, p2*, repeat from * to * 5 times, p1, (yo, p1, cddp, p1, yo, p3) × 9, yo, p1, cddp, p1, yo, p2, sm, yo, k2tog, k2.

Row 170: K4, sm, k2tog, yo, k1, yo, (cdd, yo, k1, yo) × 19 *(cdd, yo, k1, yo) × 20*, repeat from * to * 5 times, sm, k4. (569 sts)

Row 171: K2, k2tog, yo, sm, purl to 4 sts before end, sm, yo, ssk, k2.

Cast off using a very stretchy bind off of your choice (lace bind off recommended). Wet block.

Sagrada Socks

Verity Castledine

Inspired by the dice game Sagrada, where players use coloured dice to create a stained glass window, these socks feature a geometric colourwork pattern, with a cabled arch detail at the top to mimic window arches.

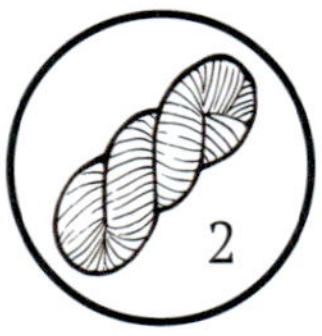

Sizes

1, (2, 3, 4)

Measurements 23 (25.5, 28, 30.5) cm/ 9 (10, 11, 12)″ circumference at ball of foot. Colourwork has limited stretch, choose the size to make considering this.

Yarns suggested

Truly Hooked standard sock in *Dark Grey* (yarn A) 100 g, approx. 425 m

And in each of *Emerald* CC1, *Cherry* CC2, *Electric Blue* CC3, *Sunshine* CC4 and *Cadbury* CC5 (colourwork yarns) 20 g of each colour, approx. 85 m.

Materials

2.5 mm (US size 2) mini circular needles (or your preferred needles) for sock knitting

Cable needle

DPNS for heel if required

Stitch markers

Waste yarn to hold heel stitches

Gauge

36 sts and 42 rows per 10 cm/4″ square in colourwork pattern when blocked. Gauge is really important for this pattern. Do swatch and block the colourwork section and adjust your needle size if need be.

The sock has an afterthought heel placed and worked at the end. The heel can be knitted in any colour.

Three colours are used per row for the main pattern, take care not to twist the yarns, and keep your floats even for a good fit.

To begin

Using yarn A, CO 72, (80, 96, 108) sts and join in the round, taking care not to twist your work, pm.

Work in rib pattern below for 12 rounds.

Size 1 and 4

k3, p3, k6, p3, k3 repeat from * to * to end of round.

Size 2 and 3

k2, p3, k6, p3, k2 repeat from * to * to end of round.

Knit 1 more row in yarn A and then proceed to chart A.

For sizes 1 and 4, use Chart A.1.

For sizes 2 and 3 use Chart A.2.

Work Chart A in full, following the correct chart for your size and introducing the colourwork yarns as indicated by the chart.

***Note**: try not to pull your floats too tight as you work. You may wish to try knitting your sock inside out, so the floats are on the outside.*

Increase round (size 1, 2 and 4 only):

With yarn A, *k9 [10, –, 27], M1*; rpt from * to * to end of round

80 (88, 96, 112) sts.

Now move to chart B. Chart B is used for all sizes.

Repeat chart B twice on the leg.

Afterthought heel setup

Using yarn A, knit 39 [43, 47, 55] sts.

Slip these 39 [43, 47, 55] heel sts from the LH needle back on to the RH needle.

Then, knit those 39 [43, 47, 55] heel sts onto waste yarn, leaving a 2–3″ tail at the start and end of your waste yarn.

Place marker at either side of the heel sts. Move onto foot instructions, and ensure you work heel instructions at the end of the pattern.

Foot

Work R1 of chart B around the foot.

Continue to work from chart B down the length of the foot until your foot measures approx. 3-4″ less than the desired length (this allows approx. 1.5–2″ for the toe and 1.5-2″ for the heel).

Toe

Break all yarns except A leaving tails for weaving in and work toe in yarn A.

Knit one round adjusting markers so you have 40 [44, 48, 56] sts on both the top and bottom of your sock.

R1: *k1, ssk, k to 3 sts before next marker, k2tog, k1, sm*; repeat from * to *.

R2: knit all sts.

Repeat R1 and R2 until you have 12 sts between the markers.   24 sts

Use Kitchener stitch to graft the toe closed.

Afterthought heel

You may wish to use DPNS to pick up the stitches.

Pick up 40 [44, 48, 56] stitches on either side of the waste yarn. Remove waste yarn and with the heel facing you, join one of your yarns on the right side. Knit a full round placing markers either side of the heel 40 [44, 48, 56] sts between each marker.

Knit 7 more rounds before decreasing the heel as follows:

R1: *k1, ssk, k to 3 sts before next marker, k2tog, k1, sm*; repeat from * to *.

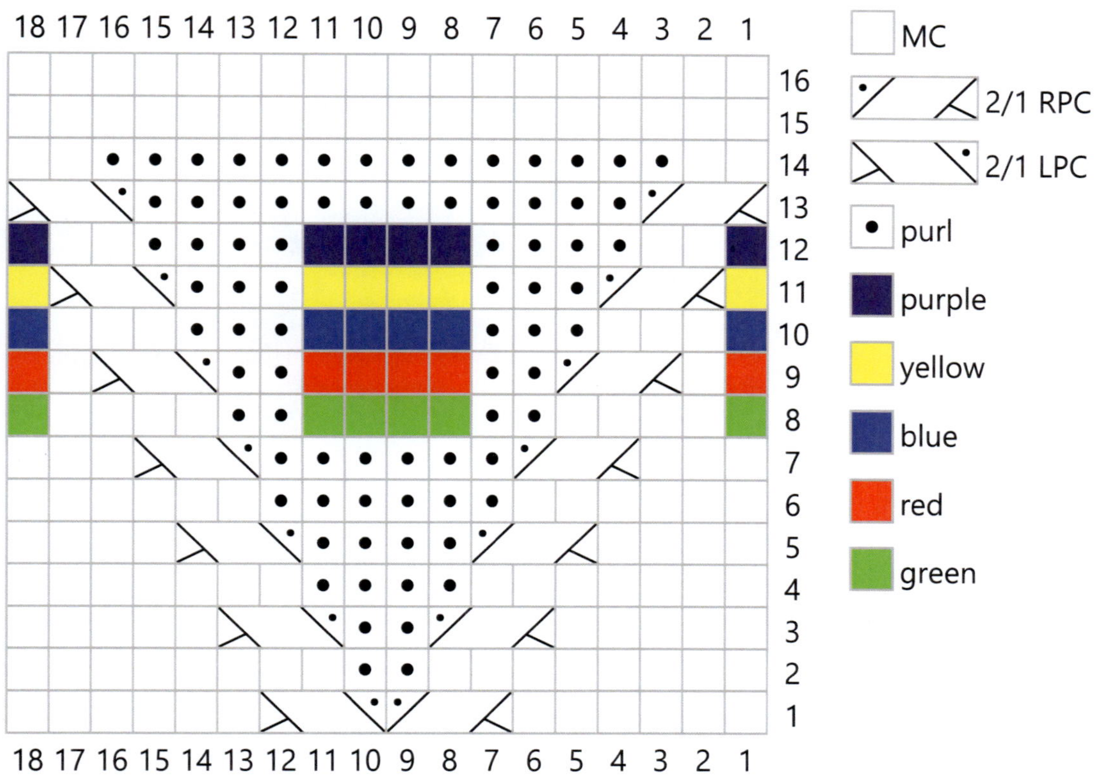

Chart A.1.

R2: knit all sts.

Repeat these two rows until you have 12 [14, 16, 18] stitches between the markers and use Kitchener stitch to graft the heel closed.

Repeat for the second sock, sew in your ends and block gently.

Chart A.1

Work colours as follows; all sts unless otherwise stated are in MC, CC sts are denoted as X CCy.

This Chart is worked over an 18 st repeat.

Round 1: K6, 2/1 RPC, 2/1 LPC, k6.

Round 2: K8, p2, k8.

Round 3: K5, 2/1 RPC, p2, 2/1 LPC, k5.

Round 4: K7, p4, k7.

Round 5: K4, 2/1 RPC, p4, 2/1 LPC, k4.

Round 6: K6, p6, k6.

Round 7: K3, 2/1 RPC, p6, 2/1 LPC, k3.

Round 8: K1 CC1, k4, p2, k4 CC1, p2, k4, k1 CC1.

Round 9: K1 CC2, k1, 2/1 RPC, p2, k4 CC2, p2, 2/1 LPC, k1, k1 CC2.

Round 10: K1 CC3, k3, p3, k4 CC3, p3, k3, k1 CC3.

Round 11: K1 CC4, 2/1 RPC, p3, k4 CC4, p3, 2/1 LPC, k1 CC4.

Round 12: K1 CC5, k2, p4, k4 CC5, p4, k2, k1 CC5.

Round 13: 2/1 RPC, p12, 2/1 LPC.

Round 14: K2, p14, k2.

Rounds 15–16: Knit.

Chart A.2

Work colours as follows; all sts unless otherwise stated are in MC, CC sts are denoted as X CCy.

This Chart is worked over a 16 st repeat.

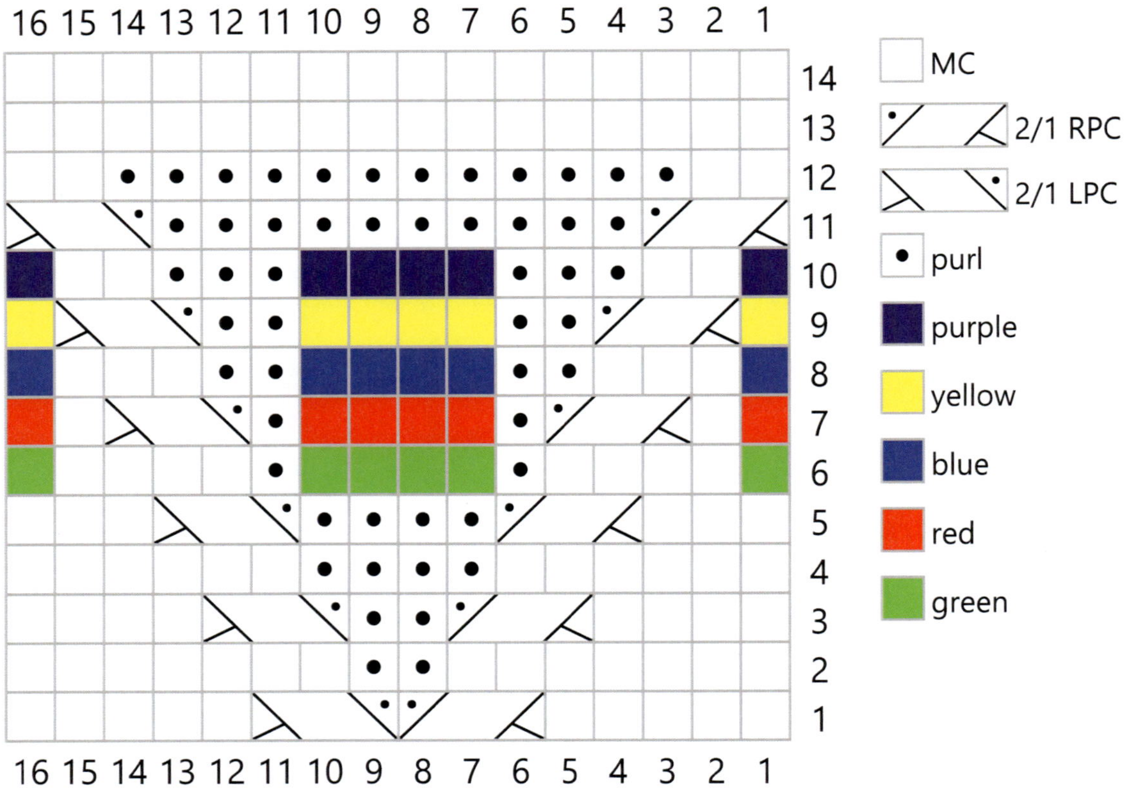

Chart A.2.

Round 1: k5, 2/1 RPC, 2/1 LPC, k5. (16 sts)

Round 2: k7, p2, k7.

Round 3: k4, 2/1 RPC, p2, 2/1 LPC, k4.

Round 4: k6, p4, k6.

Round 5: k3, 2/1 RPC, p4, 2/1 LPC, k3.

Round 6: k1 CC1, k4, p1, k4 CC1, p1, k4, K1 CC1.

Round 7: k1CC2, k1, 2/1 RPC, p1, k4 CC2, p1, 2/1 LPC, k1, k1 CC2.

Round 8: k1 CC3, k4, p2, k4 CC3, p2, k3, k1 CC3.

Round 9: k1 CC4, 2/1 RPC, p2, k4 CC4, p2, 2/1 LPC, k1 CC4.

Round 10: k1 CC5, k2, p3, k4 CC5, p3, k2, k1 CC5.

Round 11: 2/1 RPC, p3, k4, p3, 2/1 LPC.

Round 12: k2, p12, k2.

Rounds 13–14: Knit.

Chart B

As the stranded sock is worked in the round, RS facing, all sts are worked as knit unless otherwise stated.

This chart is worked over an 8 st repeat.

Round 1: Using MC, knit.

Rounds 2–4: 3 CC1, 1 MC, 3 CC2, 1 MC.

Round 5: Using MC, knit.

Rounds 6–8: 3 CC2, 1 MC, 3 CC3, 1 MC.

Round 9: Using MC, knit.

Rounds 10–12: 3 CC3, 1 MC, 3 CC4, 1 MC.

Round 13: Using MC, knit.

Rounds 14–16: 3 CC4, 1 MC, 3 CC5, 1 MC.

Round 17: Using MC, knit.

Rounds 18–20: 3 CC5, 1 MC, 3 CC1, 1 MC.

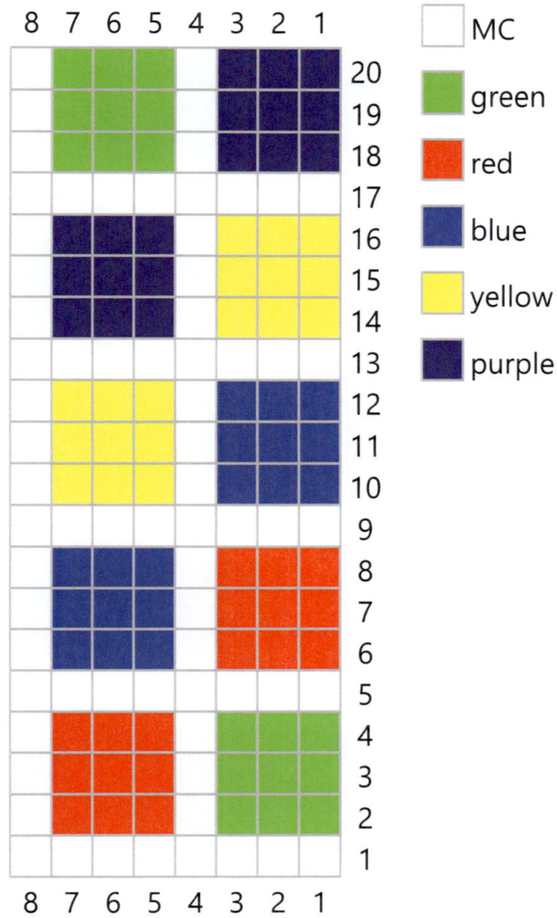
8 7 6 5 4 3 2 1
20
19
18
17
16
15
14
13
12
11
10
9
8
7
6
5
4
3
2
1
8 7 6 5 4 3 2 1
MC
green
red
blue
yellow
purple

Chart B.

Settlers Mitts

Lola Johnson

The game that put Euro games on the map for the rest of the world, where players attempt to settle the Island of Catan. An Island built of land type hexes, which are placed in a random configuration every game. These mitts echo the changing nature of the island, with the hexes you can move about and choose your own configuration, along with the road pattern across the rest of the mitts. With the option to play with colourwork and/or texture, you can build these mitts entirely your own.

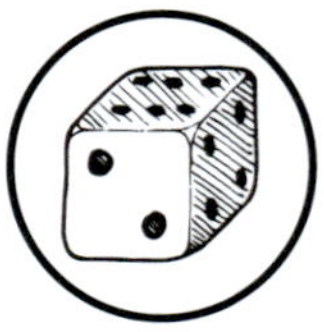

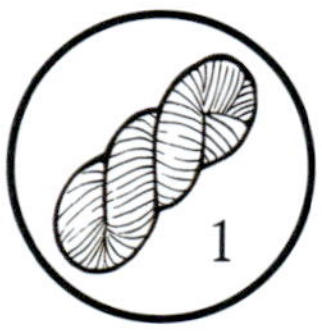

Gauge

32 sts × 40 rows stockinette stitch

Needle size

2.5–3 mm/US 1½–2 ½ to get gauge

DPNs, short circumference needles or magic loop recommended

Materials

Third Vault Yarns Companion 4 ply in *Lands of Catan Set*

Sea 200 m/50 g

Desert 20 m/5 g

Fields 20 m/5 g

Pasture 20 m/5 g

Mountain 20 m/5 g

Hills 20 m/5 g

Forest 20 m/5 g

Size

S [M/L]

The Settlers mitts pattern can be made in a number of ways – colourwork and textured hexes, colourwork and plain hexes, or as single colour mitts with the hexes for texture.

Colourwork with textured hexes

Knit the pattern as written using the hex tile charts for their texture.

Colourwork with plain hexes

Knit the pattern as written, knit plain across the hex tile sts in colour.

Single colour with texture

You can choose to change all the colourwork to texture by using the hex tile charts and when you would have used a CC purl instead. Or ignore the outside colourwork for plain mitts and only use the hex tiles texture (in this case it is recommended to place and move markers to define where your hex tiles go.

The charts for the Hand and Hex Tiles, and their write ups, can be found after the written pattern.

Construction notes

The Mitts are constructed by knitting the thumbs in the round, with the colours you would choose for the corresponding hand hex tiles. Then the hand is knit in the round up to rows 39[49] where the thumb is joined, they are knit together in one piece, in a seamless method of construction.

Both mitts and thumbs are knit in the round and as such RS facing at all times. All stitches will be knit unless worked as texture stitches.

Left thumb

CO 8 sts using Judy's Magic CO in MC.

Round 1: Using MC: Knit

Round 2: *K1, m1r*, repeat from * to * 7 times, 8 times total. (16 sts)

Round 3: *K2, m1r*, repeat from * to * 7 times. (24 sts)

For the small size use CC1

Rounds 4–5: *3 MC, 1 CC2*, repeat from * to * 5 times.

Rounds 6–7: 2 MC, *1 CC2, 3 MC* repeat from * to * 4 times, 1 CC2, 1 MC.

Round 8: 1 MC, *1 CC2, 3 MC*, repeat from * to * 4 times, 1 CC2, 2 MC.

For the small size change to CC2

Round 9: repeat round 8.

Rounds 10 & 11: *1 CC2, 3 MC*, repeat from * to * 5 times.

Rounds 12–16: Repeat rounds 4–8.

Round 17: 1 MC, *1 CC3, 3 MC*, repeat from * to * 4 times, 1 CC3, 2 MC.

Rounds 18 & 19: *1 CC3, 3 MC*, repeat from * to * 5 times.

Rounds 20–21: *3 MC, 1 CC3*, repeat from * to * 5 times.

Rounds 22–23: 2 MC, *1 CC3, 3 MC*, repeat from * to * 4 times, 1 CC3, 1 MC.

Round 24: repeat round 8.

Place stitches on waste yarn and knit left hand until round 39[49], then join thumb and knit sts to hand on round 40[50]. The two hand sts in the border should be put on waste yarn.

For the small size use the contrast colour as used for the hand sts.

Round 25: Place 1 st on waste yarn, k1 in CC3, *k3 in MC, k1 in CC3*, repeat from * to * 4 times, k1 in MC, place last st on waste yarn.   (22 sts)

Round 26: Using MC k2tog, k1 in MC, *k1 in

Left thumb chart

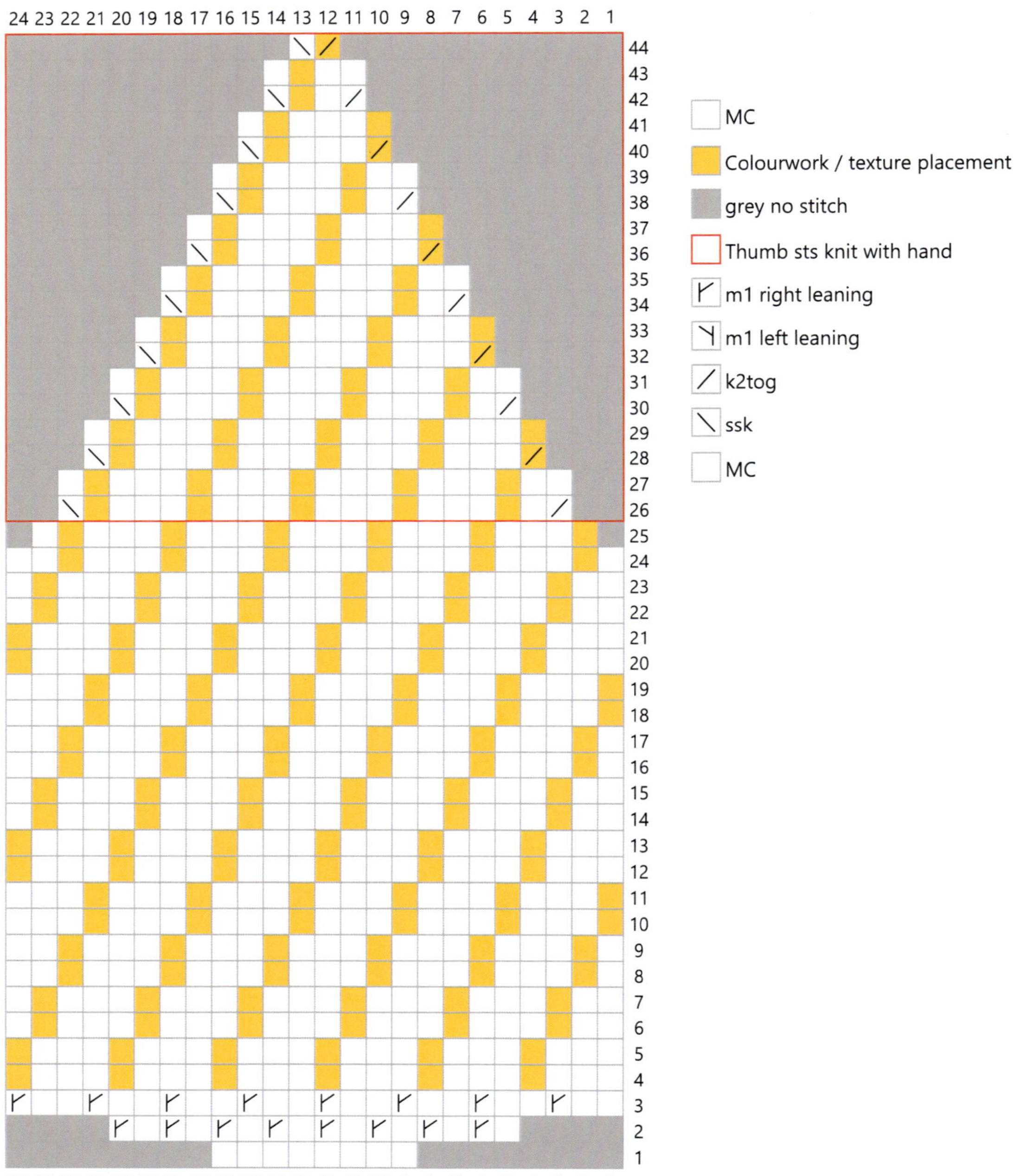

CC3, k3 in MC*, repeat from * to * 3 times, k1 in CC3, ssk in MC. (20 sts)

Round 27: 2 MC, *1 CC3, 3 MC*, repeat from * to * 3 times, 1 CC3, 1 MC.

Round 28: K2tog in CC3, *k3 in MC, k1 in CC3*, repeat from * to * 3 times, ssk in MC. (18 sts)

Round 29: *1 CC3, 3 MC*, repeat from * to * 3 times, 1 CC3, 1 MC.

Round 30: K2tog in MC, k1 in MC, *k1 in CC3, k3 in MC*, repeat from * to * 2 times, k1 in CC3, ssk in MC. (16 sts)

Round 31: 2 MC, *1 CC3, 3 MC*, repeat from * to * 2 times, 1 CC3, 1 MC.

Round 32: K2tog in CC3, *k3 in MC, k1 in CC3*, repeat from * to * 2 times, ssk in MC. (14 sts)

Round 33: *1 CC3, 3 MC*, repeat from * to * 2 times, 1 CC3, 1 MC.

Round 34: K2tog in MC, k1 in MC, *k1 in CC3, k3 in MC*, repeat from * to * once, k1 in CC3, ssk in MC. (12 sts)

Round 35: 2 MC, *1 CC3, 3 MC*, repeat from * to * once, 1 CC3, 1 MC.

Round 36: K2tog in CC3, *k3 in MC, k1 in CC3*, repeat from * to * once, ssk in MC. (10 sts)

Round 37: *1 CC3, 3 MC*, repeat from * to * once, 1 CC3, 1 MC.

Round 38: K2tog in MC, k1 in MC, k1 in CC3, k3 in MC, k1 in CC3, ssk in MC. (8 sts)

Round 39: 2 MC, 1 CC3, 3 MC, 1 CC3, 1 MC.

Round 40: K2tog in CC3, k3 in MC, k1 in CC3, ssk in MC. (6 sts)

Round 41: 1 CC3, 3 MC, 1 CC3, 1 MC.

Round 42: K2tog in MC, k1 in MC, k1 in CC3, ssk in MC. (4 sts)

Round 43: 2 MC, 1 CC3, 1 MC.

Round 44: K2tog in CC3, ssk in MC. (2 sts)

Left mitt

Add and knit from your chosen hex tiles where the pattern indicates.

Using Judy's magic cast on CO 20 sts onto two needles

Round 1: Using MC, knit. (20 sts)

Round 2: *K2, m1r* repeat from * to * 9 times, 10 times total. (30 sts)

Round 3: Knit.

Round 4: *K3, m1r* repeat from * to * 9 times. (40 sts)

Round 5: Knit.

Round 6: Using MC, k1, m1r, k1 in CC1, m1r in MC, k3, Tile Chart in CC1, k3 in MC, m1r , k1 in CC1, (m1r in MC, k1) × 2, m1r in CC1, (k4 in MC, k1 in CC1) × 3, k3 in MC, m1r in MC , k1 in CC1, m1r in MC. (48 sts)

Round 7: K2 in MC, k1 in CC1, k4 in MC, Tile Chart in CC1, *k4 in MC, k1 in CC1*, repeat from * to * 5 times, k1 in MC.

Round 8: Using MC, k1, m1r, k1, m1r in CC1, k4 in MC, Tile Chart in CC1, k4 in MC, m1r in CC1, (k1 in MC, m1r in MC) × 3, (k1 in CC1, k4 in MC) × 2, k1 in CC1, k1 in MC, (k1 in CC1, k4 in MC) × 2, m1r in CC1, k1 in MC, m1r in MC. (56 sts)

Round 9: K1 in MC, m1r in MC, k2 in MC, k1 in CC1, k4 in MC, Tile Chart in CC1, k4 in MC, k1 in CC1, (k2 in MC, m1r in MC) × 2, k2 in MC, (k1 in CC1, k4 in MC) × 2, k1 in CC1, k1 in MC, (k1 in CC1, k4 in MC) × 2, k1 in CC1, k2 in MC, m1r in MC. (60 sts)

Round 10: K1 in CC1, m1r in MC, k2 in MC, k1 in CC1, k4 in MC, Tile Chart in CC1, k4 in MC, k1 in CC1, k2 in MC, m1r in MC, k2 in CC1, m1r in MC, k2 in MC, (k1 in CC1, k4 in MC) × 2, k1 in CC1, k3 in MC, (k1 in CC1, k4 in MC) × 2, k1 in CC1, k2 in MC, m1r in MC. (64 sts)

Round 11: 1 CC1, 3 MC, 1 CC1, 4 MC, Tile Chart in CC1, 4 MC, 1 CC1, 3 MC, 2 CC1, *3 MC, (1 CC1, 4 MC) × 2, 1 CC1*, repeat from * to * once, 3 MC .

Rounds 12–13: 3 MC, 1 CC1, 4 MC, Tile Chart in CC1, 4 MC, 1 CC1, 6 MC, (1 CC1, 4 MC) × 2, 1 CC1, 5 MC, (1 CC1, 4 MC) × 2, 1 CC1, 2 MC .

Rounds 14–15: 2 MC, 1 CC1, 4 MC, Tile Chart in CC1, (4 MC, 1 CC1) × 4, (3 MC, 1 CC1) × 2, (4 MC, 1 CC1) × 2, 1 MC .

Rounds 16–17: 3 MC, 1 CC1, 4 MC, Tile Chart in CC1, 4 MC, 1 CC1, 6 MC, (1 CC1, 4 MC) × 2, 1 CC1, 5 MC, (1 CC1, 4 MC) × 2, 1 CC1, 2 MC .

Rounds 18–19: 1 CC1, 3 MC, 1 CC1, 4 MC, Tile Chart in CC1, 4 MC, 1 CC1, 3 MC, 2 CC1, *3 MC, (1 CC1, 4 MC) × 2, 1 CC1*, repeat from * to * once, 3 MC .

Rounds 20–21: (1 CC1, 4 MC) × 2, Tile Chart in CC1, 4 MC, 1 CC1, 4 MC, 2 CC1, (4 MC, 1 CC1) × 3, 1 MC, (1 CC1, 4 MC) × 3.

Round 22: 1 MC, (1 CC1, 4 MC) × 2, Tile Chart in CC1, (4 MC, 1 CC1) × 2, 2 MC, (1 CC1, 4 MC) × 6, 1 CC1.

Round 23: 1 MC, (1 CC1, 4 MC) × 2, Tile Chart in CC1, (4 MC, 1 CC1) × 2, 2 MC, (1 CC1, 4 MC) × 6, 1 CC1.

Round 24: 1 MC, (1 CC2, 4 MC) × 2, Tile Chart in CC2, (4 MC, 1 CC2) × 2, 2 MC, (1 CC2, 4 MC) × 6, 1 CC2.

Round 25: 1 MC, (1 CC1, 4 MC) × 2, Tile Chart in CC2, (4 MC, 1 CC1) × 2, 2 MC, (1 CC1, 4 MC) × 6, 1 CC1.

Rounds 26–27: (1 CC2, 4 MC) × 2, Tile Chart in CC2, 4 MC, 1 CC2, 4 MC, 2 CC2, (4 MC, 1 CC2) × 3, 1 MC, (1 CC2, 4 MC) × 3.

Rounds 28–29: 1 CC2, 3 MC, 1 CC2, 4 MC, Tile Chart in CC2,, 4 MC, 1 CC2, 3 MC, 2 CC2, *3 MC, (1 CC2, 4 MC) × 2, 1 CC2*, repeat from * to * once, 3 MC.

Rounds 30–31: 3 MC, 1 CC2, 4 MC, Tile Chart in CC2, 4 MC, 1 CC2, 6 MC, (1 CC2, 4 MC) × 2, 1 CC2, 5 MC, (1 CC2, 4 MC) × 2, 1 CC2, 2 MC.

Rounds 32–33: 2 MC, 1 CC2, 4 MC, Tile Chart in CC2, (4 MC, 1 CC2) × 4, (3 MC, 1 CC2) × 2, (4 MC, 1 CC2) × 2, 1 MC.

Rounds 34–35: 3 MC, 1 CC2, 4 MC, Tile Chart in CC2, 4 MC, 1 CC2, 6 MC, (1 CC2, 4 MC) × 2, 1 CC2, 5 MC, (1 CC2, 4 MC) × 2, 1 CC2, 2 MC.

Rounds 36–37: 1 CC2, 3 MC, 1 CC2, 4 MC, Tile Chart in CC2, 4 MC, 1 CC2, 3 MC, 2 CC2, *3 MC, (1 CC2, 4 MC) × 2, 1 CC2*, repeat from * to * once, 3 MC

Rounds 38–39: (1 CC2, 4 MC) × 2, Tile Chart in CC2, 4 MC, 1 CC2, 4 MC, 2 CC2, (4 MC, 1 CC2) × 3, 1 MC, (1 CC2, 4 MC) × 3.

For the small size join for the thumb gusset here using thumb that is already knit.

Round 40: 1 MC, (1 CC1, 4 MC) × 2, Tile Chart in CC2, (4 MC, 1 CC1) × 2, SLTC [2 MC], (1 CC1, 4 MC) × 6, 1 CC1.

Round 41: 1 MC, (1 CC2, 4 MC) × 2, Tile Chart in CC2, (4 MC, 1 CC2) × 2, SLTC [2 MC], (1 CC2, 4 MC) × 6, 1 CC2.

Round 42: 1 MC, (1 CC3, 4 MC) × 2, Tile Chart in CC3, (4 MC, 1 CC3) × 2, SLTC [2 MC], (1 CC3, 4 MC) × 6, 1 CC3.

Round 43: 1 MC, (1 CC1, 4 MC) × 2, Tile Chart in CC3, (4 MC, 1 CC1) × 2, SLTC [2 MC], (1 CC1, 4 MC) × 6, 1 CC1.

Rounds 44–45: (1 CC3, 4 MC) × 2, Tile Chart in CC3, 4 MC, 1 CC3, 4 MC, SLTC [2 CC3], (4 MC, 1 CC3) × 3, 1 MC, (1 CC3, 4 MC) × 3.

Rounds 46–47: 1 CC3, 3 MC, 1 CC3, 4 MC, Tile Chart in CC3, 4 MC, 1 CC3, 3 MC, SLTC [2 CC3], *3 MC, (1 CC3, 4 MC) × 2, 1 CC3*, repeat from * to * once, 3 MC.

Small size

Rounds 48–49: 3 MC, 1 CC3, 4 MC, Tile Chart in CC3, 4 MC, 1 CC3, 2 MC, SLTC, 2MC (1 CC3, 4 MC) × 2, 1 CC3, 5 MC, (1 CC3, 4 MC) × 2, 1 CC3, 2 MC.

Medium/large size

Rounds 48–49: 3 MC, 1 CC3, 4 MC, Tile Chart in CC3, 4 MC, 1 CC3, 6 MC, (1 CC3, 4 MC) × 2, 1 CC3, 5 MC, (1 CC3, 4 MC) × 2, 1 CC3, 2 MC .

For the medium/large size join for the thumb gusset here using thumb that is already knit.

Rounds 50–51: 2 MC, 1 CC3, 4 MC, Tile Chart in CC3, 4 MC, 1 CC3, 1 MC, Left Thumb Chart, 1 MC, (1 CC3, 4 MC) × 2, (1 CC3, 3 MC) × 2, (1 CC3, 4 MC) × 2, 1 CC3, 1 MC.

Rounds 52–53: 3 MC, 1 CC3, 4 MC, Tile Chart in CC3, 4 MC, 1 CC3, 2 MC, Left Thumb Chart, 2 MC, (1 CC3, 4 MC) × 2, 1 CC3, 5 MC, (1 CC3, 4 MC) × 2, 1 CC3, 2 MC .

Rounds 54–55: 1 CC3, 3 MC, 1 CC3, 4 MC, Tile Chart in CC3, 4 MC, 1 CC3, 3 MC, Left Thumb Chart, *3 MC, (1 CC3, 4 MC) × 2, 1 CC3*, repeat from * to * once, 3 MC.

Rounds 56–57: (1 CC3, 4 MC) × 2, Tile Chart in CC3, 4 MC, 1 CC3, 4 MC, Left Thumb Chart, (4 MC, 1 CC3) × 3, 1 MC, (1 CC3, 4 MC) × 3.

Round 58: 1 MC, (1 CC3, 4 MC) × 2, Tile Chart in CC3, 4 MC, 1 CC3, 5 MC, Left Thumb Chart, 5 MC, (1 CC3, 4 MC) × 5, 1 CC3.

Round 59: 1 MC, (1 CC3, 4 MC) × 2, Tile Chart in CC3, 4 MC, 1 CC3, 5 MC, Left Thumb Chart, 5 MC, (1 CC3, 4 MC) × 5, 1 CC3.

For the small size, continue from round 70 and decrease 6 times in total on that round. Place the extra decreases somewhat centrally to the front and the back.

Rounds 60–61: 1 MC, (1 CC3, 4 MC) × 2, 1 CC3, 3 MC, 2 CC3, 3 MC, 1 CC3, 4 MC, 1 CC3, 5 MC, Left Thumb Chart, 5 MC, (1 CC3, 4 MC) × 5, 1 CC3.

Rounds 62–63: 1 CC3, (4 MC, 1 CC3) × 2, 4 MC, 2 CC3, (4 MC, 1 CC3) × 2, 4 MC, Left Thumb Chart, (4 MC, 1 CC3) × 3, 1 MC, (1 CC3, 4 MC) × 3.

Rounds 64–65: 1 CC3, 3 MC, (1 CC3, 4 MC) × 2, 1 CC3, 2 MC, (1 CC3, 4 MC) × 2, 1 CC3, 3 MC, Left Thumb Chart, *3 MC, (1 CC3, 4 MC) × 2, 1 CC3*, repeat from * to * once, 3 MC.

Rounds 66–67: 3 MC, (1 CC3, 4 MC) × 5, 1 CC3, 2 MC, Left Thumb Chart, 2 MC, (1 CC3, 4 MC) × 2, 1 CC3, 5 MC, (1 CC3, 4 MC) × 2, 1 CC3, 2 MC .

Round 68: K2tog in MC, (k1 in CC3, k4 in MC) × 2, k1 in CC3, k6 in MC, (k1 in CC3, k4 in MC) × 2, k1 in CC3, k1 in MC, Left Thumb Chart, k1 in MC, (k1 in CC3, k4 in MC) × 2, (k1 in CC3, k3 in MC) × 2, (k1 in CC3, k4 in MC) × 2, ssk in CC3. (62 sts)

Round 69: 1 MC, (1 CC3, 4 MC) × 2, 1 CC3, 6 MC, (1 CC3, 4 MC) × 2, 1 CC3, 1 MC, 2 CC3, 1 MC, (1 CC3, 4 MC) × 2, (1 CC3, 3 MC) × 2, (1 CC3, 4 MC) × 2, 1 CC3.

Round 70: Using MC, *k2tog, k26, ssk*, repeat from * to * once. (56 sts)

Round 71: Knit.

Round 72: *K2tog, k24, ssk* repeat from * to * once. (52 sts)

Rounds 73–83: Knit.

Round 84: Purl.

Rounds 85–96: Knit.

Cast off using a stretchy bind off, turn rounds 85–96 inwards and sew the bind off to row 73.

Graft/ Kitchener the hand sts and thumb sts on waste yarn together.

Right thumb

CO 8 sts using Judy's Magic CO in MC

Round 1: Knit

Round 2: *M1l, k1*, repeat from * to * 7 times, 8 times total. (16 sts)

Round 3: *M1l, k2*, repeat from * to * 7 times. (24 sts)

For the small size use CC4

Round 4: (1 CC5, 3 MC) × 6.

Round 5: repeat round 4.

Round 6: 1 MC, (1 CC5, 3 MC) × 5, 1 CC5, 2 MC.

Round 7: repeat round 6.

Round 8: 2 MC, (1 CC5, 3 MC) × 5, 1 CC5, 1 MC.

For the small size change to CC5

Round 9: repeat round 8.

Rounds 10 & 11: (3 MC, 1 CC5) × 6.

Rounds 12–16: Repeat rounds 4–8.

Round 17: 2 MC, (1 CC6, 3MC) × 5, 1 CC6, 1 MC.

Rounds 18 & 19: (3 MC, 1 CC6) × 6.

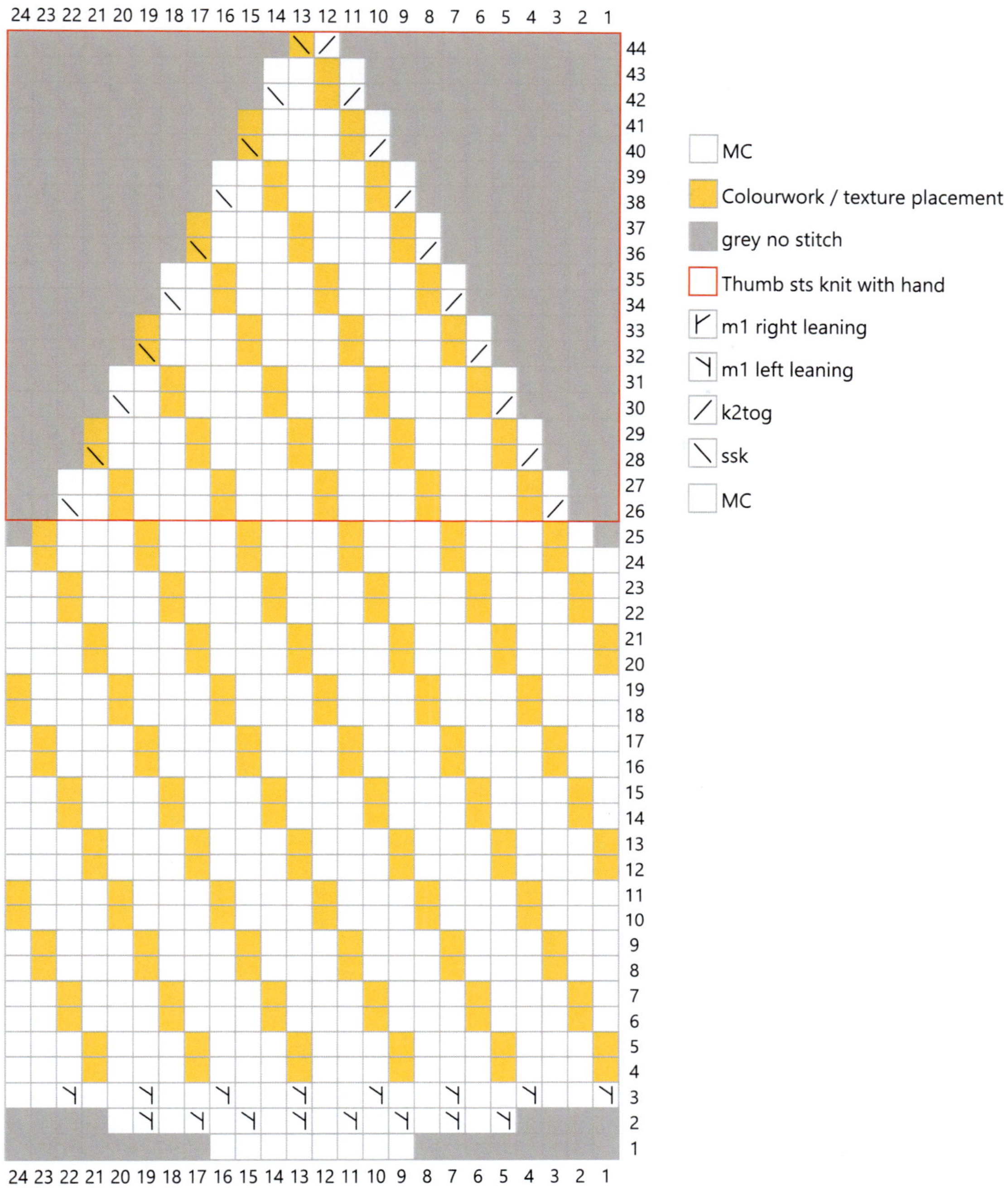

Right thumb chart

Rounds 20 & 21: (1 CC6, 3 MC) × 6.

Rounds 22 & 23: 1 MC, (1 CC6, 3 MC) × 5, 1 CC6, 2 MC.

Round 24: repeat round 8.

Place stitches on waste yarn and knit Right hand until round 39[49], then join thumb and knit sts along in hand on round 40[50]. The two hand sts in the border should be put on waste yarn.

For the small size use the contrast colour as used for the hand sts.

Round 25: Place 1 st on waste yarn, k1 in MC (k1 in CC6, k3 in MC) × 5, k1 in CC6, place last st on waste yarn. (22 sts)

Round 26: K2tog in MC, (k1 in CC6, k3 in MC) × 4, k1 in CC6, k1 in MC, ssk in MC. (20 sts)

Round 27: 1 MC, (1 CC6, 3 MC) × 4, 1 CC6, 2 MC.

Round 28: K2tog in MC, (k1 in CC6, k3 in MC) × 4, ssk in CC6. (18 sts)

Round 29: 1 MC, (1 CC6, 3 MC) × 4, 1 CC6.

Round 30: K2tog in MC, (k1 in CC6, k3 in MC) × 3, k1 in CC6, k1 in MC, ssk in MC. (16 sts)

Round 31: 1 MC, (1 CC6, 3 MC) × 3, 1 CC6, 2 MC.

Round 32: K2tog in MC, (k1 in CC6, k3 in MC) × 3, ssk in CC6. (14 sts)

Round 33: 1 MC, (1 CC6, 3 MC) × 3, 1 CC6.

Round 34: K2tog in MC, (k1 in CC6, k3 in MC) × 2, k1 in CC6, k1 in MC, ssk in MC. (12 sts)

Round 35: 1 MC, (1 CC6, 3 MC) × 2, 1 CC6, 2 MC.

Round 36: K2tog in MC, (k1 in CC6, k3 in MC) × 2, ssk in CC6. (10 sts)

Round 37: 1 MC, (1 CC6, 3 MC) × 2, 1 CC6.

Round 38: K2tog in MC, k1 in CC6, k3 in MC, k1 in CC6, k1 in MC, ssk in MC. (8 sts)

Round 39: 1 MC, 1 CC6, 3 MC, 1 CC6, 2 MC.

Round 40: K2tog in MC, k1 in CC6, k3 in MC, ssk in CC6. (6 sts)

Round 41: 1 MC, 1 CC6, 3 MC, 1 CC6.

Round 42: K2tog in MC, k1 in CC6, k1 in MC, ssk in MC. (4 sts)

Round 43: 1 MC, 1 CC6, 2 MC.

Round 44: K2tog in MC, ssk in CC6. (2 sts)

Right mitt

Add and knit from your chosen hex tiles where the pattern indicates.

Round 1: Using MC, knit. (20 sts)

Round 2: *M1l, k2* repeat from * to * 9 times. (30 sts)

Round 3: knit.

Round 4: *M1l, k3* repeat from * to * 9 times. (40 sts)

Round 5: knit.

Round 6: M1l in MC, k1 in CC4, m1l in MC, k3 in MC, (k1 in CC4, k4 in MC) × 3, m1l in CC4, (k1 in MC, m1l in MC) × 2, k1 in CC4, m1l in MC, k3 in MC, Tile Chart in CC4, k3 in MC, m1l in MC, k1 in CC4, m1l in MC, k1 in MC. (48 sts)

Round 7: 1 MC, (1 CC4, 4 MC) × 6, Tile Chart in CC4, 4 MC, 1 CC4, 2 MC.

Round 8: Using MC, M1l, k1, m1l in CC4, (k4 in MC, k1 in CC4) × 2, k1 in MC, (k1 in CC4, k4 in MC) × 2, k1 in CC4, (m1l in MC, k1 in MC) × 3, m1l in CC4, k4 in MC, Tile Chart in CC4, k4 in MC, m1l in CC4, k1 in MC, m1l in MC, k1 in MC. (56 sts)

Round 9: Using MC, M1l, k2, (k1 in CC4, k4 in MC) × 2, k1 in CC4, k1 in MC, (k1 in CC4, k4 in

MC) × 2, k1 in CC4, (k2 in MC, m1l in MC) × 2, k2 in MC, k1 in CC4, k4 in MC, Tile Chart in CC4, k4 in MC, k1 in CC4, k2 in MC, m1l in MC, k1 in MC. (60 sts)

Round 10: Using MC, M1l, k2, (k1 in CC4, k4 in MC) × 2, k1 in CC4, k3 in MC, (k1 in CC4, k4 in MC) × 2, k1 in CC4, k2 in MC, m1l in MC, k2 in CC4, m1l in MC, k2 in MC, k1 in CC4, k4 in MC, Tile Chart in CC4, k4 in MC, k1 in CC4, k2 in MC, m1l in MC, k1 in CC4. (64 sts)

Round 11: (3 MC, (1 CC4, 4 MC) × 2, 1 CC4) × 2, 3 MC, 2 CC4, 3 MC, 1 CC4, 4 MC, Tile Chart in CC4, 4 MC, 1 CC4, 3 MC, 1 CC4.

Rounds 12–13: 2 MC, (1 CC4, 4 MC) × 2, 1 CC4, 5 MC, (1 CC4, 4 MC) × 2, 1 CC4, 6 MC, 1 CC4, 4 MC, Tile Chart in CC4, 4 MC, 1 CC4, 3 MC.

Rounds 14–15: 1 MC, (1 CC4, 4 MC) × 2, (1 CC4, 3 MC) × 2, (1 CC4, 4 MC) × 4, Tile Chart in CC4, 4 MC, 1 CC4, 2 MC.

Rounds 16–17: 2 MC, (1 CC4, 4 MC) × 2, 1 CC4, 5 MC, (1 CC4, 4 MC) × 2, 1 CC4, 6 MC, 1 CC4, 4 MC, Tile Chart in CC4, 4 MC, 1 CC4, 3 MC.

Rounds 18–19: (3 MC, (1 CC4, 4 MC) × 2, 1 CC4) × 2, 3 MC, 2 CC4, 3 MC, 1 CC4, 4 MC, Tile Chart in CC4, 4 MC, 1 CC4, 3 MC, 1 CC4.

Rounds 20–21: (4 MC, 1 CC4) × 3, 1 MC, (1 CC4, 4 MC) × 3, 2 CC4, 4 MC, 1 CC4, 4 MC, Tile Chart in CC4, (4 MC, 1 CC4) × 2.

Round 22: (1 CC4, 4 MC) × 6, 1 CC4, 2 MC, (1 CC4, 4 MC) × 2, Tile Chart in CC4, (4 MC, 1 CC4) × 2, 1 MC.

Round 23: (1 CC4, 4 MC) × 6, 1 CC4, 2 MC, (1 CC4, 4 MC) × 2, Tile Chart in CC4, (4 MC, 1 CC4) × 2, 1 MC.

Round 24: (1 CC5, 4 MC) × 6, 1 CC5, 2 MC, (1 CC5, 4 MC) × 2, Tile Chart in CC5, (4 MC, 1 CC5) × 2, 1 MC.

Round 25: repeat round 22.

Rounds 26–27: (4 MC, 1 CC5) × 3, 1 MC, (1 CC5, 4 MC) × 3, 2 CC5, 4 MC, 1 CC5, 4 MC, Tile Chart in CC5, (4 MC, 1 CC5) × 2.

Rounds 28–29: (3 MC, (1 CC5, 4 MC) × 2, 1 CC5) × 2, 3 MC, 2 CC5, 3 MC, 1 CC5, 4 MC, Tile Chart in CC5, 4 MC, 1 CC5, 3 MC, 1 CC5.

Rounds 30–31: 2 MC, (1 CC5, 4 MC) × 2, 1 CC5, 5 MC, (1 CC5, 4 MC) × 2, 1 CC5, 6 MC, 1 CC5, 4 MC, Tile Chart in CC5, 4 MC, 1 CC5, 3 MC.

Rounds 32–33: 1 MC, (1 CC5, 4 MC) × 2, (1 CC5, 3 MC) × 2, (1 CC5, 4 MC) × 4, Tile Chart in CC5, 4 MC, 1 CC5, 2 MC.

Rounds 34–35: 2 MC, (1 CC5, 4 MC) × 2, 1 CC5, 5 MC, (1 CC5, 4 MC) × 2, 1 CC5, 6 MC, 1 CC5, 4 MC, Tile Chart in CC5, 4 MC, 1 CC5, 3 MC.

Rounds 36–37: (3 MC, (1 CC5, 4 MC) × 2, 1 CC5) × 2, 3 MC, 2 CC5, 3 MC, 1 CC5, 4 MC, Tile Chart in CC5, 4 MC, 1 CC5, 3 MC, 1 CC5.

Rounds 38–39: (4 MC, 1 CC5) × 3, 1 MC, (1 CC5, 4 MC) × 3, 2 CC5, 4 MC, 1 CC5, 4 MC, Tile Chart in CC5, (4 MC, 1 CC5) × 2.

For the small size join for the thumb gusset here using thumb that is already knit.

Round 40: (1 CC5, 4 MC) × 6, 1 CC5, SRTC [2 MC], (1 CC5, 4 MC) × 2, Tile Chart in CC5, (4 MC, 1 CC5) × 2, 1 MC.

Round 41: (1 CC5, 4 MC) × 6, 1 CC5, SRTC [2 MC], (1 CC5, 4 MC) × 2, Tile Chart in CC5, (4 MC, 1 CC5) × 2, 1 MC.

Round 42: (1 CC6, 4 MC) × 6, 1 CC6, SRTC [2 MC], (1 CC6, 4 MC) × 2, Tile Chart in CC6, (4 MC, 1 CC6) × 2, 1 MC.

Round 43: (1 CC6, 4 MC) × 6, 1 CC6, SRTC [2 MC], (1 CC6, 4 MC) × 2, Tile Chart in CC6, (4 MC, 1 CC6) × 2, 1 MC.

Rounds 44–45: (4 MC, 1 CC6) × 3, 1 MC, (1 CC6, 4 MC) × 3, SRTC [2 CC6], 4 MC, 1 CC6, 4 MC, Tile Chart in CC6, (4 MC, 1 CC6) × 2.

Rounds 46–47: (3 MC, (1 CC6, 4 MC) × 2, 1 CC6) × 2, 3 MC, SRTC [2 CC6], 3 MC, 1 CC6, 4 MC, Tile Chart in CC6, 4 MC, 1 CC6, 3 MC, 1 CC6.

Small size

Rounds 48–49: 2 MC, (1 CC6, 4 MC) × 2, 1 CC6, 5 MC, (1 CC6, 4 MC) × 2, 1 CC6, 2 MC, SRTC, 2 MC, 1 CC6, 4 MC, Tile Chart in CC6, 4 MC, 1 CC6, 3 MC.

Medium/large size

Rounds 48–49: 2 MC, (1 CC6, 4 MC) × 2, 1 CC6, 5 MC, (1 CC6, 4 MC) × 2, 1 CC6, 6 MC, 1 CC6, 4 MC, Tile Chart in CC6, 4 MC, 1 CC6, 3 MC.

For the medium/large size join for the thumb gusset here using thumb that is already knit.

Rounds 50–51: 1 MC, (1 CC6, 4 MC) × 2, (1 CC6, 3 MC) × 2, (1 CC6, 4 MC) × 2, 1 CC6, 1 MC, Right Thumb Chart, 1 MC, 1 CC6, 4 MC, Tile Chart in CC6, 4 MC, 1 CC6, 2 MC.

Rounds 52–53: 2 MC, (1 CC6, 4 MC) × 2, 1 CC6, 5 MC, (1 CC6, 4 MC) × 2, 1 CC6, 2 MC, Right Thumb Chart, 2 MC, 1 CC6, 4 MC, Tile Chart in CC6, 4 MC, 1 CC6, 3 MC.

Rounds 54–55: (3 MC, (1 CC6, 4 MC) × 2, 1 CC6) × 2, 3 MC, Right Thumb Chart, 3 MC, 1 CC6, 4 MC, Tile Chart in CC6, 4 MC, 1 CC6, 3 MC, 1 CC6.

Rounds 56–57: (4 MC, 1 CC6) × 3, 1 MC, (1 CC6, 4 MC) × 3, Right Thumb Chart, 4 MC, 1 CC6, 4 MC, Tile Chart in CC6, (4 MC, 1 CC6) × 2.

Round 58: (1 CC6, 4 MC) × 5, 1 CC6, 5 MC, Right Thumb Chart, 5 MC, 1 CC6, 4 MC, Tile Chart in CC6, (4 MC, 1 CC6) × 2, 1 MC.

Round 59: (1 CC6, 4 MC) × 5, 1 CC6, 5 MC, Right Thumb Chart, 5 MC, 1 CC6, 4 MC, Tile Chart in CC6, (4 MC, 1 CC6) × 2, 1 MC.

For the small size, continue from round 70 and decrease 6 times in total on that round. Place the extra decreases somewhat centrally to the front and the back.

Rounds 60–61: (1 CC6, 4 MC) × 5, 1 CC6, 5 MC, Right Thumb Chart, 5 MC, 1 CC6, 4 MC, 1 CC6, 3 MC, 2 CC6, 3 MC, (1 CC6, 4 MC) × 2, 1 CC6, 1 MC.

Rounds 62–63: (4 MC, 1 CC6) × 3, 1 MC, 1 CC6, (4 MC, 1 CC6) × 2, 4 MC, Right Thumb Chart, 4 MC, 2 CC6, (4 MC, 1 CC6) × 3.

Rounds 64–65: (3 MC, (1 CC6, 4 MC) × 2, 1 CC6) × 2, 3 MC, Right Thumb Chart, 3 MC, (1 CC6, 4 MC) × 2, 1 CC6, 2 MC, (1 CC6, 4 MC) × 2, 1 CC6, 3 MC, 1 CC6.

Rounds 66–67: 2 MC, (1 CC6, 4 MC) × 2, 1 CC6, 5 MC, (1 CC6, 4 MC) × 2, 1 CC6, 2 MC, Right Thumb Chart, 2 MC, (1 CC6, 4 MC) × 5, 1 CC6, 3 MC.

Round 68: K2tog in CC6, (k4 in MC, k1 in CC6) × 2, (k3 in MC, k1 in CC6) × 2, (k4 in MC, k1 in CC6) × 2, k1 in MC, Right Thumb Chart, k1 in MC, (k1 in CC6, k4 in MC) × 2, k1 in CC6, k6 in MC, (k1 in CC6, k4 in MC) × 2, k1 in CC6, ssk in MC.

Round 69: (1 CC6, 4 MC) × 2, (1 CC6, 3 MC) × 2, (1 CC6, 4 MC) × 2, 1 CC6, 1 MC, Right Thumb Chart, 1 MC, (1 CC6, 4 MC) × 2, 1 CC6, 6 MC, (1 CC6, 4 MC) × 2, 1 CC6, 1 MC.

Round 70: Using MC, *k2tog, k26,ssk*, repeat from * to * once. (56 sts)

Round 71: Knit.

Round 72: *K2tog, k24, ssk* repeat from * to * once. (52 sts)

Rounds 73–83: Knit.

Round 84: Purl.

Rounds 85–96: Knit.

Cast off using a stretchy bind off, turn rounds 85–96 inwards and sew the bind off to row 73.

Graft/Kitchener the hand sts and thumb sts on waste yarn together.

Block both mitts.

- MC
- grey no stitch
- Colourwork/texture placement
- 1st Hex Tile
- 2nd Hex Tile
- 3rd Hex Tile
- Small Thumb Gusset
- M/L Thumb Gusset
- p2tog
- p2tog tbl
- m1 purlwise left leaning
- m1 purlwise right leaning
- m1 left leaning
- m1 right leaning
- ssk
- k2tog
- purl

Mitt Charts Key (over the page)

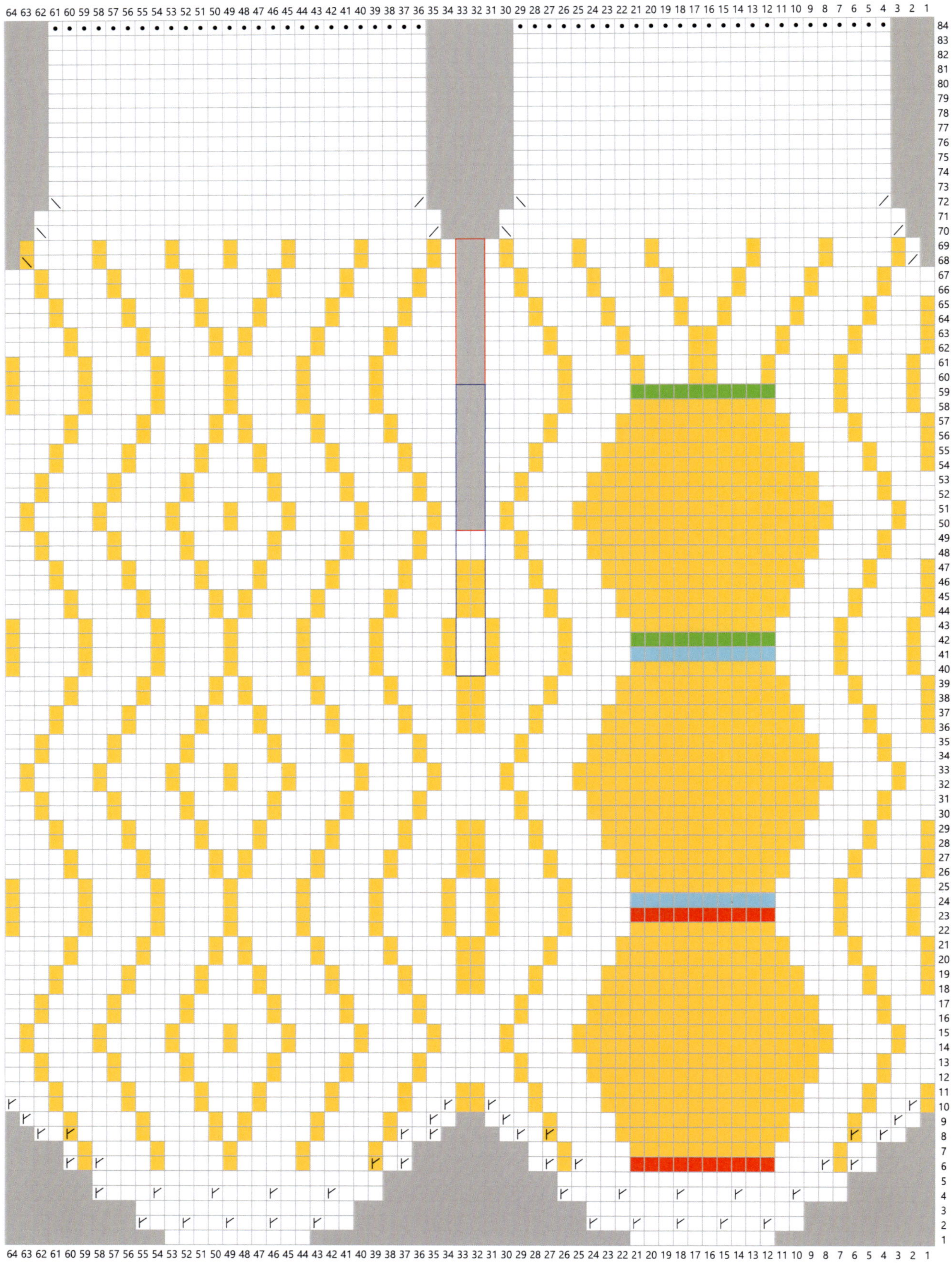

Left Mitt Chart

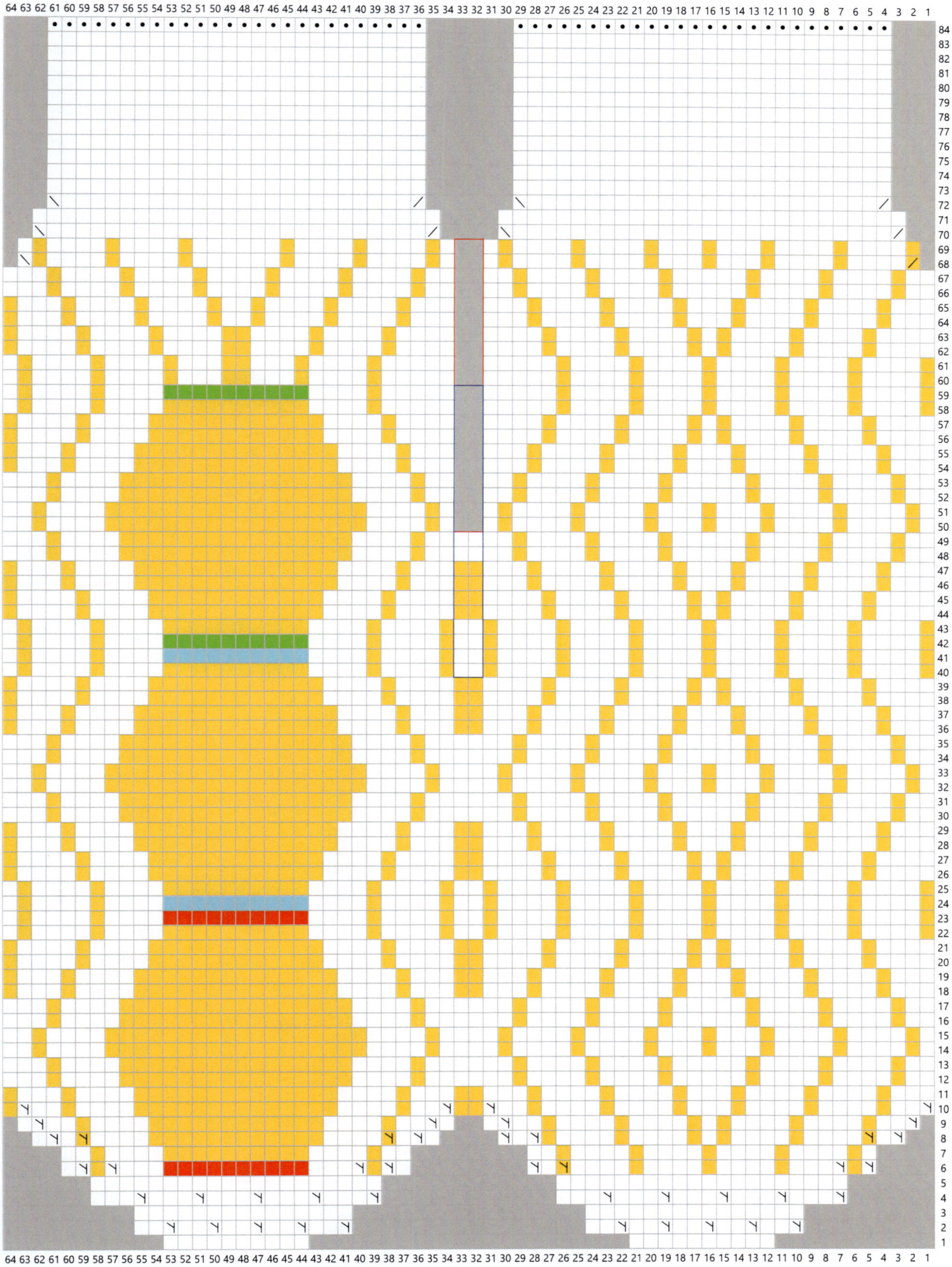

Right Mitt Chart

Hex Tiles

Desert

Round 1: Knit. (10 sts)
Round 2: K2, p3, k3, p2.
Round 3: K1, p1, k2, (p3, k1) × 2. (12 sts)
Round 4: P2, k3, p5, k2.
Round 5: K1, p3, k3, p4, k3. (14 sts)
Round 6: (K2, p3) × 2, k2, p2.
Round 7: K3, p2, k3, (p3, k1) × 2. (16 sts)
Round 8: (K2, p3) × 3, k1.
Round 9: (K2, p3) × 3, k3. (18 sts)
Round 10: K1, (p3, k2) × 2, p4, k3.
Round 11: P2, k2, p4, k2, p3, k3. (16 sts)
Round 12: P1, k2, p6, k2, p3, k2.
Round 13: K1, (p3, k2) × 2, p3. (14 sts)
Round 14: P3, k4, p3, k2, p2.
Rounds 15–16: P2, k4, p3, k3. (12 sts)
Round 17: K4, p3, k3. (10 sts)
Round 18: K3, p3, k4.

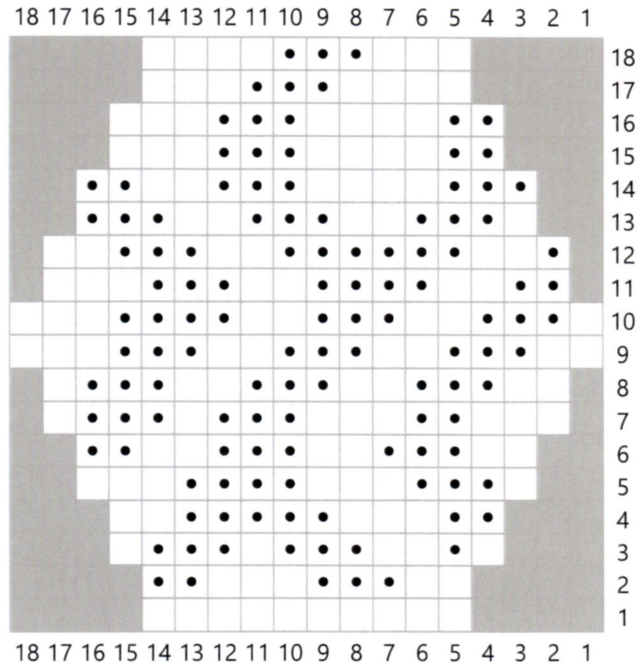

RS: knit
WS: purl

• RS: purl
WS: knit

grey no stitch

Pasture

Round 1: Knit. (10 sts)
Round 2: (K1, p1) × 5.
Round 3: (K1, p1) × 5, k2. (12 sts)
Round 4: (P1, k1) × 6.
Round 5: K2, (p1, k1) × 6. (14 sts)
Round 6: (K1, p1) × 7.
Round 7: (K1, p1) × 7, k2. (16 sts)
Round 8: (P1, k1) × 8.
Round 9: K2, (p1, k1) × 8. (18 sts)
Round 10: (K1, p1) × 9.
Round 11: (K1, p1) × 8. (16 sts)
Round 12: Repeat round 8.
Round 13: (P1, k1) × 7. (14 sts)
Round 14: Repeat round 6.
Round 15: (K1, p1) × 6. (12 sts)
Round 16: Repeat round 4.
Round 17: (P1, k1) × 5. (10 sts)
Round 18: Repeat round 2.

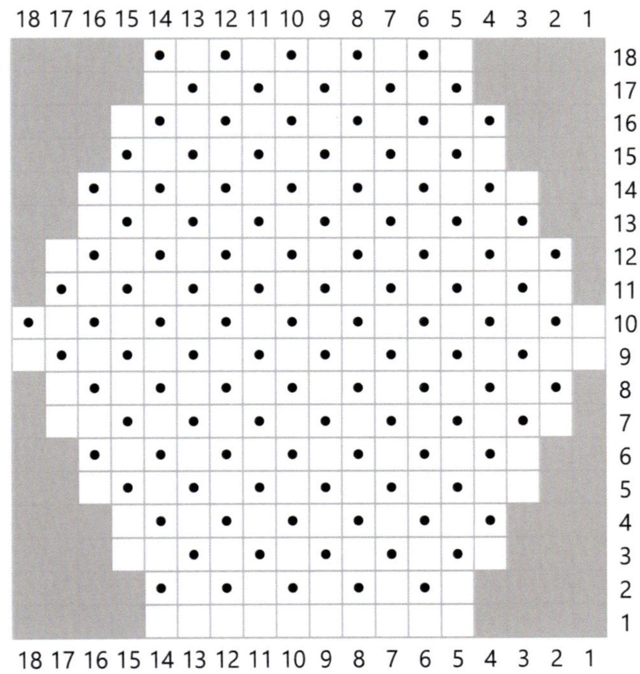

Mountain

Round 1: Knit. (10 sts)
Round 2: K4, p4, k2.
Round 3: K3, p2, k1, p4, k2. (12 sts)
Round 4: K2, p3, k1, p5, k1.
Round 5: K3, p2, k2, p5, k2. (14 sts)
Round 6: K2, p2, k4, p5, k1.
Round 7: K10, p5, k1. (16 sts)
Round 8: K12, p4.
Round 9: K3, p1, k10, p3, k1. (18 sts)
Round 10: K2, p3, k9, p4.
Round 11: P7, k7, p2. (16 sts)
Round 12: P7, k9.
Round 13: P7, k7. (14 sts)
Round 14: P8, k6.
Rounds 15–16: P8, k4. (12 sts)
Rounds 17–18: Purl. (10 sts)

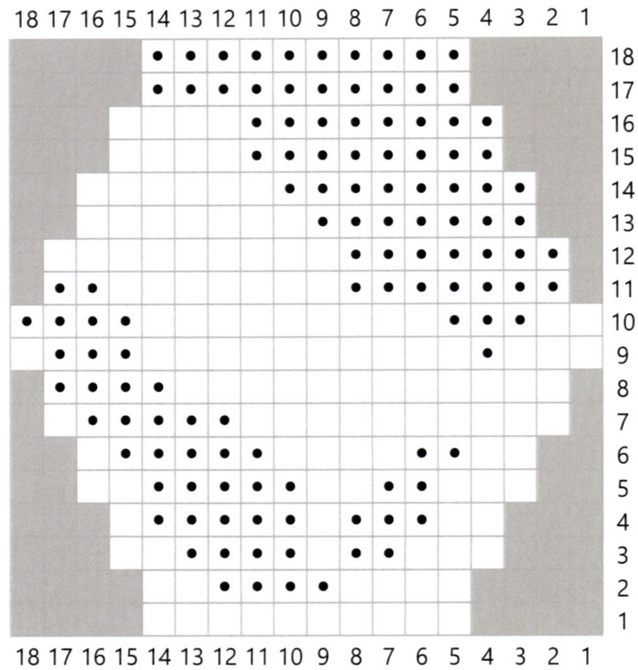

RS: knit
WS: purl

grey no stitch

RS: purl
WS: knit

Visualise Knit sts

Forest

The green sts within the chart are to aid visualisation of the knit sts amongst the purl, there is no additional colour change.

Round 1: Knit. (10 sts)
Round 2: P4, k2, p4.
Round 3: K1, p3, k1, p2, k1, p3, k1. (12 sts)
Round 4: P3, k1, p1, k2, p1, k1, p3.
Round 5: K1, p3, k1, p1, k2, p1, k1, p3, k1. (14 sts)
Round 6: P5, k1, p2, k1, p5.
Round 7: K1, (p2, k2) × 3, p2, k1. (16 sts)
Round 8: (P2, k1) × 2, p4, (k1, p2) × 2.
Round 9: (K1, p1) × 2, k2, p1, k1, p2, k1, p1, k2, (p1, k1) × 2. (18 sts)
Round 10: (P2, k1, p1, k2, p1, k1) × 2, p2.
Round 11: Repeat round 8. (16 sts)
Round 12: P3, (k2, p2) × 2, k2, p3.
Round 13: Repeat round 6. (14 sts)
Round 14: P4, k1, p1, k2, p1, k1, p4.
Round 15: Repeat round 4. (12 sts)
Round 16: P4, k1, p2, k1, p4.
Round 17: Repeat round 2. (10 sts)
Round 18: Purl.

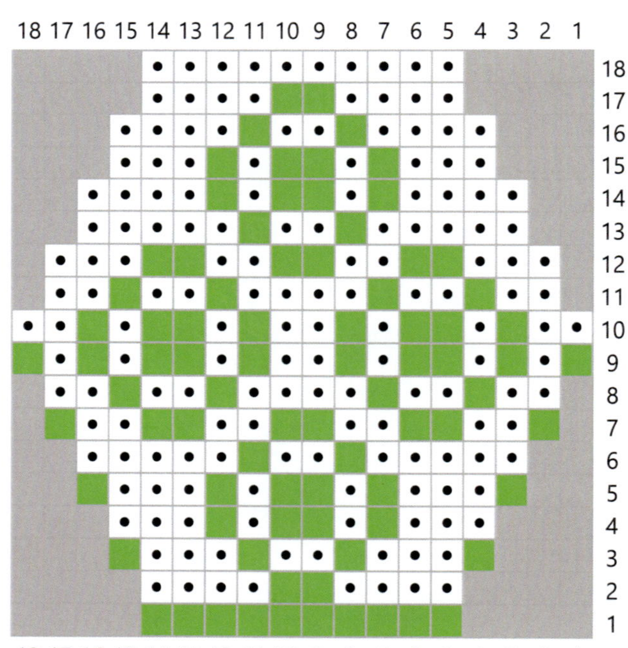

Field

Round 1: Knit. (10 sts)
Round 2: K2, (p1, k1) × 2, p1, k3.
Round 3: K4, (p1, k1) × 2, p1, k3. (12 sts)
Round 4: K1, p1, k3, (p1, k1) × 2, p1, k2.
Round 5: (K1, p1) × 2, k3, (p1, k1) × 2, p1, k2. (14 sts)
Round 6: (P1, k1) × 2, p1, k3, (p1, k1) × 3.
Round 7: K2, (p1, k1) × 2, p1, k3, (p1, k1) × 3. (16 sts)
Round 8: (K3, (p1, k1) × 2, p1) × 2.
Round 9: (K1, p1, k3, p1, k1, p1) × 2, k2. (18 sts)
Round 10: (P1, k1, p1, k3, p1, k1) × 2, p1, k1.
Round 11: (P1, k1, p1, k3, p1, k1) × 2. (16sts)
Round 12: ((K1, p1) × 2, k3, p1) × 2.
Round 13: Repeat round 5. (14 sts)
Round 14: K2, p1, k1, p1, k3, (p1, k1) × 3.
Round 15: (P1, k1) × 2, p1, k3, (p1, k1) × 2. (12 sts)
Round 16: (K1, p1) × 3, k3, p1, k1, p1.
Round 17: (K1, p1) × 3, k3, p1. (10 sts)
Round 18: Repeat round 2.

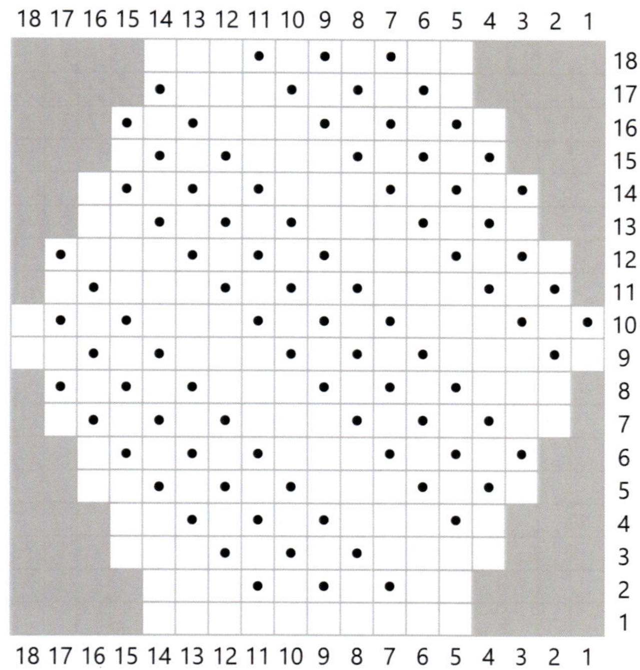

RS: knit
WS: purl

RS: purl
WS: knit

grey no stitch

Hills

Round 1: Knit. (10 sts)
Round 2: P1, k5, p4.
Round 3: K1, p2, k4, p4, k1. (12 sts)
Round 4: P4, k3, p5.
Round 5: K1, p5, k1, p3, k4. (14 sts)
Round 6: P9, k5.
Round 7: K1, p8, k7. (16 sts)
Round 8: P2, k3, p3, k4, p4.
Round 9: K1, p2, k4, p2, k3, p5, k1. (18 sts)
Round 10: P1, k7, p2, k1, p7.
Round 11: K9, p7. (16 sts)
Round 12: K7, p5, k3, p1.
Round 13: K5, p5, k4. (14 sts)
Round 14: K2, p3, k1, p2, k6.
Round 15: P5, k7. (12 sts)
Round 16: P6, k6.
Round 17: P6, k4. (10 sts)
Round 18: Purl.

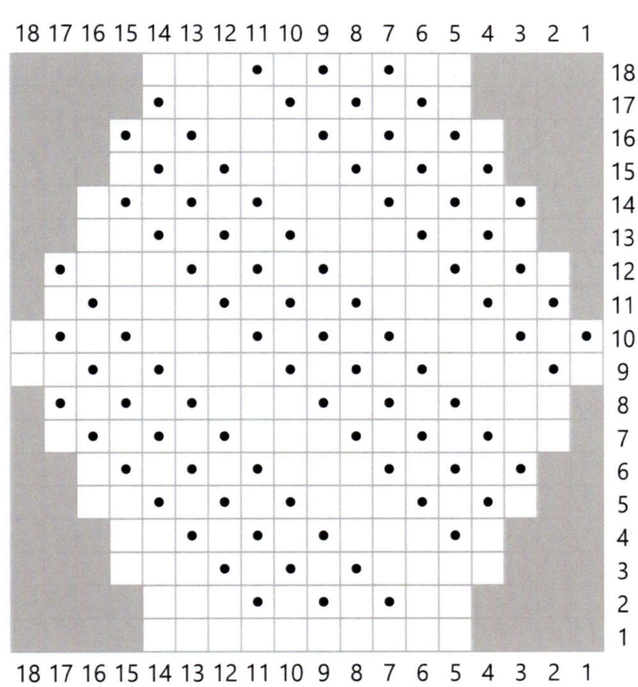

Thematic Games

Thematic Games, as the name suggests, emphasise theme to create a more dramatic atmosphere in gaming, with focus on characters, individual traits and a moderate to high level of luck. Usually these games have a focus on player conflict, however the majority of the games we've chosen here demonstrate a player(s) versus the game element, allowing for some co-operative strategy to be introduced into play. To represent these games we've designed a selection of patterns focusing on building techniques, with twisted knitting, short rows, slip stitches and colourwork, whilst still being quick knits.

ApoCowlypse

Lola Johnson

Dice rolls and co-operative strategy in a post-zombie apocalyptic world. You play as survivors, working to escape to a safer place, collect food, find other survivors and more. ApoCowlypse was designed for a post-apocalyptic aesthetic, something quick and light weight that can be worn in a number of ways to keep you warm. Using twisted knitting to add structure and short rows for shaping. It's a project that lets you try out some new techniques whilst still being a relatively simple and fast knit.

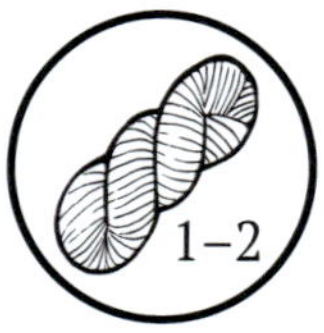

Sizes

Adjustable

Yarn

Third Vault Yarns Tesseract in *Zombicide* 600 m/100 g 1–2 skeins approx.

Or fingering weight yarn with a put up of 400 m/100 g can be used for a thicker fabric.

Yarn usage by Smallest to Largest variations 200–300 m/50g to 600–900 m/150 g (estimate).

Any type of yarn can be used for this: wool, wool blends or non wool; however, the closer neckline requires a lot of stretch, so wool is a better option for this variation.

Needle size

5.5 mm/US 9 suggested with cable 40–100 cm/16″–40″

Gauge – blocked

14 sts by 24 rows 10 cm/4″ stockinette

16 sts by 36 rows 10 cm/4″ Twisted Knitting

Sizing

This cowlette is very adaptable, you can make changes to sizing based on the width and the length of it at several points. It is designed to be worn in 3 different ways – with the longest edge draped at the side, to the front or to the back, giving an asymmetrical look; a draped circular shawl look; or a capelet style.

The depth (A) will be set by how many short row sections you work, follow the instructions in the pattern to work a depth of 37–58 cm/14″–23″. This is directly linked to the length of the placket (B). The depth will also affect the circumference (D) if following the pattern exactly as written.

It is possible to increase the depth of the cowlette (A and B) without increasing the circumference (D) by working the short row shaping without increasing on the intervening rounds.

The neck width is the circumference of the initial starting row, (determined by the style of neck you choose in the pattern) and the placket width (C). Circumference (D) is determined by the number of increases you choose to do times depth (A) plus the placket width you choose (C).

For best results pick measurements that will result in at least 2″–15″ ease for you. This is determined by your neck circumference, and body width at your upper chest including your arms. Use the sizing table overleaf to help determine the best sizing options for you.

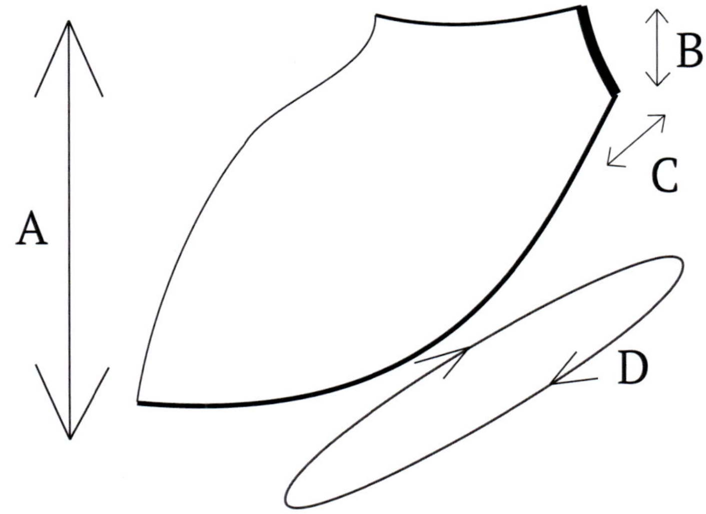

Cowlette shape and structure

A – Longest edge	B – Placket Length	Size range fits (body width)	C – Placket width	Neck circumference	D – Circumference incl. placket width
Standard (Deeper) cowl neck					*Size One [Two]*
37 cm/14.5″ (47cm 18.5″)	10 cm/4″ (20 cm/8″)	Smallest (92–147 cm/37″–59″)	8 cm/3″, 12 sts	46 cm/18″ 53 cm/21″	127 cm/51″ [152 cm/61″]
43 cm/17″ (53 cm/21″)	13 cm/5″ (23 cm/9″)	(as above)	10 cm/4″, 16 sts	48 cm/19″ 56 cm/22″	132 cm/53″ [168 cm/67″]
48 cm/19″ (58 cm/23″)	15 cm/6″ (25.5 cm/10″)	Largest (111–193 cm/44″–77″)	13 cm/5″, 20 sts	51 cm/20″ 58 cm/23″	142 cm/57″ [183 cm/73″]
					149 cm/59″ [198 cm/78″]

Sizing table

Smocked stitch patterning

This can be added randomly to make your version unique. The stitch pattern is over one row and four stitches. It is recommended not to add too many smocked stitches close together or on a row, as it will create a tighter fabric. Keep the insertion of these stitches random and with good spacing between them. You can make the decision on where you'd like to place them to provide different looks.

On a knit row:

- Insert the right hand needle between the 4th and 5th sts on the left hand needle.
- Wrap the yarn around the RH needle, and pull it through as if to knit.
- Place the loop created on the LH needle.
- K2tog the first two sts on the LH needle
- Continue in stockinette.

Placket

Row 1: *From between the next 2 sts, knit 1 st through the bar, slip the next st purlwise*, repeat from * to * {12/16/20} times total.

Row 2: *K2tog (the st knitted from below and the slipped st)*, repeat from * to * {12/16/20} times total.

Choose your neckline preference, Closer or Wider.

Closer neck set up

CO 50 sts + {12/16/20} sts

Join in the round being careful not to twist.

Round 1: Place marker, knit to marker.

Round 2: Slip marker, purl to marker.

Round 3: Sm, knit to marker.

Round 4: Repeat round 2.

Round 5: Sm, knit {12/16/20}, pm, knit to marker.

Skip rounds 6 to 27 and work rounds 28 and 29 then continue to the first short row section if you would prefer to go straight into the shawl style shaping.

Round 6: Sm, {Placket Row 1}, sm, knit to marker.

Round 7: Sm, {Placket Row 2}, sm, knit to marker.

Rounds 8–27: Repeat rounds 6 and 7.

Round 28: Sm, {Placket Row 1}, sm, k1, Left lifted increase, knit 24 sts, LLI, knit to 1 st before marker, LLI, k1. (53 sts + {12/16/20} sts)

Round 29: Sm, {Placket Row 2}, sm, ***k4, LLI*** repeat to last st, k1. (66 sts + {12/16/20} sts)

Wider neck set up

CO 66 + {12/16/20} sts

Join in the round being careful not to twist.

Round 1: Place marker, knit to marker.

Round 2: Slip marker, purl to marker.

Round 3: Sm, knit to marker.

Round 4: Repeat round 2.

Round 5: Sm, knit [12/16/20], pm, knit to marker.

Skip rounds 6 to 29 if you would prefer to go straight into the shawl style shaping and continue to the first short row section.

Round 6: Sm, {Placket Row 1}, sm, knit to marker.

Round 7: Sm, {Placket Row 2}, sm, knit to marker.

Rounds 8–29: Repeat rounds 6 and 7.

(1) Short row section

These short rows are written for the German short row method. Please see the techniques section. The numbers that correspond to ***X***, ***Y*** and ***Z*** can be found in the short row number chart at the end.

Short Row 1: Sm, {Placket Row 1} sm, knit to ***X*** sts before the next marker, turn work.

Short Row 2: Purl to ***X*** sts before the next marker, turn work.

Short Row 3: Knit to ***Y*** sts before the last turn, turn work.

Short Row 4: Purl to ***Y*** sts before the last turn, turn work.

Short Row 5: Knit to ***Z*** sts before the last turn, turn work.

Short Row 6: Purl to ***Z*** sts before the last turn, turn work.

Short Row 7: Knit to marker (knitting the double sts as 1 st).

Round 7: Sm, {Placket Row 2}, Sm, knit to marker (knitting the double sts as 1 st).

Continue with pattern

Round 8: Sm, {Placket Row 1}, sm, ***k5, LLI*** repeat to last st, k1. (79 sts + {12/16/20} sts)

Round 9: Sm, {Placket Row 2}, sm, knit to marker.

(2) Work Short Row Section as before.

Round 12: Sm, {Placket Row 1}, sm, ***k6, LLI***, repeat to last st, k1. (92 sts + {12/16/20} sts)

Round 13: Repeat round 9

(3) Work Short Row Section as before.

Round 16: Sm, {Placket Row 1}, sm, ***k7, LLI***, repeat to last st, k1. (105 sts + {12/16/20} sts)

Round 17: Repeat round 9

(4) Work Short Row Section as before.

From this point on you can adjust the circumference (D on schematic) by working the increases for smaller[larger] size.

Round 20: Sm, {Placket Row 1}, sm, ***k8[5], LLI***, repeat to last st[end of round], k1[0]. (118[126] sts+ {12/16/20} sts)

Round 21: Repeat round 9

(5) Work Short Row Section as before.

Round 24: Sm, {Placket Row 1}, sm, ***k9[6], LLI***, repeat to last st[end of round], k1[0]. (131[147] sts + {12/16/20} sts)

Round 25: Repeat round 9

(6) Work Short Row Section as before.

Round 28: Sm, {Placket Row 1}, sm, ***k10[7], LLI***, repeat to last st[end of round], k1[0]. (144[168] sts + {12/16/20} sts)

Round 29: Repeat round 9

(7) Work Short Row Section as before.

Round 32: Sm, {Placket Row 1}, sm, ***k11[8], LLI***, repeat to last st[end of round], k1[0]. (157[189] sts + {12/16/20} sts)

Round 33: Repeat round 9

(8) Work Short Row Section as before.

Round 36: Sm, {Placket Row 1}, sm, ***k12[9], LLI***, repeat to last st[end of round], k1[0]. (170[210] sts + {12/16/20} sts)

Round 37: Repeat round 9

For a length of 37 cm/14.5″ (47 cm/18.5″) on the longest edge, move to finishing from here. At any point from here, you can choose to make the increase rows plain rows, to maintain the same width to a desired length.

50[60]″ + placket width

(9) Work Short Row Section as before.

Round 40: Sm, {Placket Row 1}, sm, ***k13[10], LLI***, repeat to last st[end of round], k1[0]. (183[231] sts + {12/16/20} sts)

Round 41: Repeat round 9

52[66]″ + placket width

(10) Work Short Row Section as before.

Round 44: Sm, {Placket Row 1}, sm, ***k14[11], LLI***, repeat to last st[end of round], k1[0]. (196[252] sts + {12/16/20} sts)

Round 45: Repeat round 9

56[72]″ + placket width

For a length of 43 cm/17″ (53 cm/21″) on the longest edge, move to finishing from here.

(11) Work Short Row Section as before.

Round 48: Sm, {Placket Row 1}, sm, ***k15[12], LLI***, repeat to last st[end of round], k1[0]. (209[273] sts + {12/16/20} sts)

Round 49: Repeat round 9

59[78]″ + placket width

(12) Work Short Row Section as before.

This end point will give you a length of 48 cm/19″ (58 cm/23″) on the longest edge.

Finishing

Round 1: Sm, knit to marker, sm, knit to marker.

Round 2: Sm, purl to marker, sm, purl to marker.

Round 3: Repeat round 1.

Round 4: Repeat round 2.

Cast off using lace bind off, and wet block.

	1	2	3	4	5	6	7	8	9	10	11	12
X	7	8	10	10	11[10]	12[14]	13[16]	15[20]	17[22]	20[24]	20[26]	22[30]
Y	7	8	10	11	12[12]	13[16]	15[17]	17[22]	19[24]	20[26]	20[26]	22[30]
Z	7	8	10	11	13[14]	14[18]	17[18]	17[24]	19[24]	20[26]	20[26]	22[30]

Short Row Number Chart

King of All Hats

Lola Johnson

Claiming Tokyo or New York is the aim of the game this King of all Hats is inspired by, and of course being the last monster standing. Some simple slip stitch colourwork creates the energy cube lookalike structure and then some stranded colourwork to show off the faces of the special die in the game. Whilst this hat won't make you a monarch it's certainly an adornment on your crown that will make you stand out!

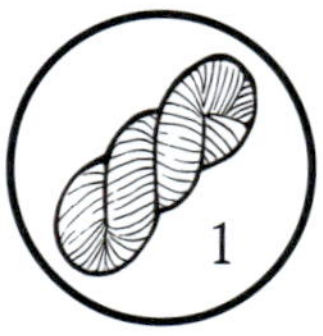

Gauge

20 sts × 24 rows stocking st in 10 cm/4″

Sizing

45 [48, 54, 57] cm/18 [19, 21.5, 23]″
hat circumference

For a snug fit choose a size approximately 2 cm/0.75″ smaller than your head measurement.

Yarn

Third Vault Yarns Caroline Dk in *Big Monster Energy Duo* 230 m/115 g, 100% superwash merino, 50 g of each colour.

Needles

4 mm/US 6 circular needles 40 cm/16″

Notions

6 × stitch markers

Needle for sewing in ends

Special stitches

K1 uls: Knit 1 under loose strand.

Insert needle under loose strand, knit next st and bring completed stitch out under the loose strand to catch strand behind stitch.

Brim

Cast on 90[96,108,114] using MC.

Knit in 1 × 1 (p1, k1) rib for 4 cm/1.5″ in MC.

Body

When finishing a row with the MC leave your working yarn in front, and do not tuck it behind. It will be needed to keep the pattern uninterrupted for the next slip st row.

Round 1: Using MC, *k1, sl5 wyif*, repeat from * to * 14[15,17,18] times. (This is 15[16,18,19] repeats in total.)

Rounds 2 & 3: Using CC, knit to end.

Round 4: Using MC, sl 2 wyif, k1 uls, *sl 5 wyif, k1 uls*, repeat from * to * 13[14,16,17] times, sl 2 wyif, k1.

Rounds 5 & 6: Repeat rounds 2 and 3.

Round 7: Using MC, k1 uls, *sl 5 wyif, k1 uls; rep from * to last 6 sts, sl 5 wyif.

Repeat rounds 2–7 until you reach 15 cm/6″ from the start of the ribbing. For a slouchier hat knit to 18 or 20 cm/7″ or 8″ from the start of the ribbing before you decrease.

Place your MC to the back of work, it will now be on the inside of the hat, you will need it to begin stranded knitting for the crown shaping. Knit one round in CC, then k2, k1 uls, *k5, k1 uls*, repeat from * to * 13[14,16,17] times, k3.

Crown

It is possible to knit this without the stranded colourwork, by following only the decrease stitches, and knitting the rest as plain knitting. You can then, if you wish, follow the charts visually to duplicate stitch (sew) the motifs on to the crown of the hat.

90[96,108,114] sts

Round 0: Using CC, knit round, placing a stitch marker after every 15[16,18,19] sts,

The order of faces is Life, Attack and Energy, repeated.

Work colours as follows; all sts unless otherwise stated are in CC, MC sts are denoted as ***X*** in MC.

Round 1: *Ssk, k7[8,9,10], k1 in MC, k5[5,6,6], sm, ssk, k7[8,9,10], k2 in MC, k4[4,5,5], sm, ssk, k10[11,12,13], k1 in MC, k2[2,3,3]*, repeat from * to *. (84,90,102, 108 sts)

Round 2: *K7[8,9,10], k3 in MC, k4[4,5,5], sm, k7[8,9,10], k4 in MC, k3[3,4,4], sm, k10[11,12,13], k2 in MC, k2[2,3,3]*, repeat from * to *.

Round 3: *Ssk, k4[5,6,7], k5 in MC, k3[3,4,4], sm, ssk, k5[6,7,8], k4 in MC, k3[3,4,4], sm, ssk, k7[8,9,10], k2 in MC, k3[3,5,4]*, repeat from * to *. (78,84,96,102 sts)

Round 4: *K5[6,7,8], k5 in MC, k3[3,4,4], sm, k7[8,9,10], k3 in MC, k1, k1 in MC, k1[1,2,2], sm, k7[8,9,10], k2 in MC, k4[4,5,5]*, repeat from * to *.

Round 5: *Ssk, k2[3,4,5], k7 in MC, k2[2,3,3], sm, ssk, k3[4,5,6], k1 in MC, k5, k1 in MC, k1[1,2,2], sm, ssk, k5[6,7,8], k4 in MC, k2[2,3,3]*, repeat from * to *. (72,78,90, 96 sts)

Round 6: *Ssk, k2[3,4,5], k2 in MC, k1, k2 in MC, k3[3,4,4], sm, ssk, k1[2,3,4], k2 in MC, (k1, k1 in MC) × 2, k3[3,4,4], sm, ssk, k6[7,8,9], k2 in MC, k2[2,3,3]*, repeat from * to *. (66,72,84,90 sts)

Round 7: *K3[4,5,6], k2 in MC, k1, k2 in MC, k3[3,4,4], sm, k5[6,7,8], k1 in MC, k1, k1 in MC, k3[3,4,4], sm, k6[7,8,9], k2 in MC, k3[3,4,4]*, repeat from * to *.

For the next 2 rounds the energy bolt is the only motif still using the MC, it is advisable to either wrap the MC around your CC every few sts to avoid long floats, or use the intarsia method for the last 4 sts on each of the motifs.

Round 8: *Ssk, k9[10,12,13], sm, ssk, k9[10,12,13], sm, ssk, k3[4,5,6], k2 in MC, k4[4,5,5]*, repeat from * to *. (60[66,78, 84] sts)

Round 9: *Ssk, k8[9,11,12], sm, ssk, k8[9,11,12], sm, ssk, k1[2,3,4], k2 in MC, k5[5,6,6]*, repeat from * to *. (54[60,72, 78] sts)

Round 10: *Ssk, k3[3,4,5], ssk, k2[3,4,4], sm*, repeat from * to * 5 times. (42[48,60, 66] sts)

Size 18"/45 cm and 19"/48 cm

Round 11: *Ssk, k5[6]* repeat from * to * 5 more times. (36[42] sts)

Size 18"/45.5 cm only:

Round 12: *Ssk, k1* repeat from * to * 11 more times. (24 sts)

Round 13: *Ssk* repeat from * to * 11 more times. (12 sts)

Sizes 19"/48 cm to 23"/58.5 cm

Round 11: *Ssk, k[2,3,4], ssk, k[1,3,3]* repeat from * to * 5 more times. (30, 48, 54 sts)

Round 12: *Ssk, k[1,2,3], ssk, k[0,2,2]* repeat from * to * 5 more times. (18, 36, 42 sts)

Last round for 19"/48 cm only:

Round 13: *Ssk, k1* repeat from * to * 5 more times. (12 sts)

All other sizes:

Round 13: *Ssk, k[1,2], ssk, k[1,1]* repeat from * to * 5 more times. (24, 30 sts)

Last round for 21.5"/54.5 cm

Round 14: *Ssk, k[0,1], ssk* repeat from * to * 5 more times. (12, 18 sts)

Last round for 23"/58.5 cm

Round 15: *Ssk, k1* repeat from * to * 5 more times. (12 sts)

Leave a tail and break yarn, thread yarn through remaining stitches. Pull tight, bringing the tail to the inside of the hat. Weave in ends and block.

These charts are a visual aid so you can see the motifs, they are accurate charts of the decreases for the smallest size.

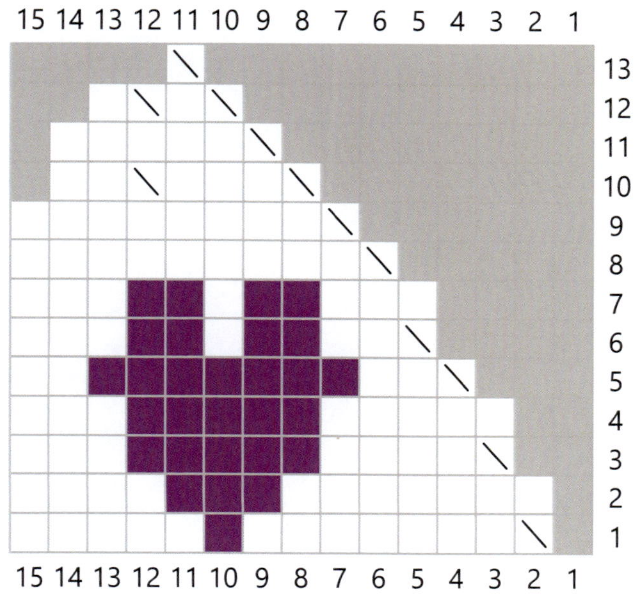

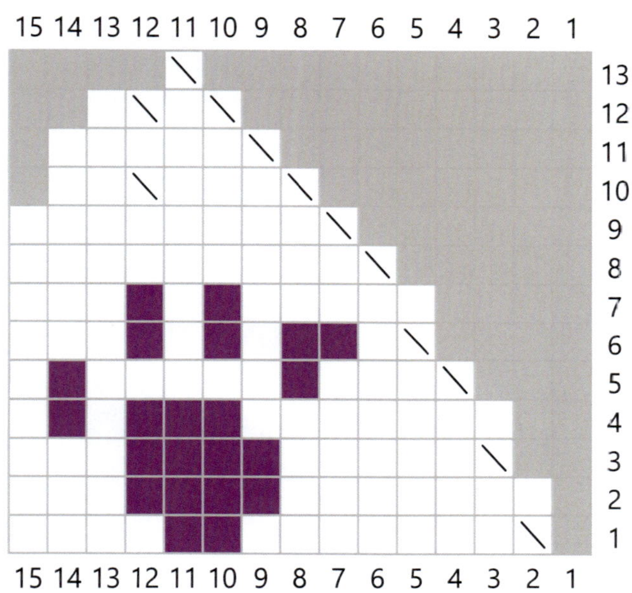

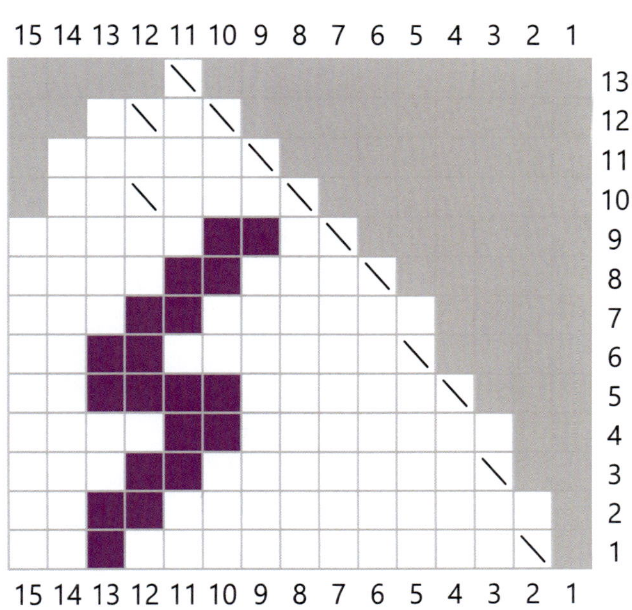

Mindreaper Mitts

Angelina Panozzo

Breaking seals and summoning the elder gods is the aim of the game, to rid this world of them once and for all. These mitts show the encroaching war on the psyche from those betentacled gods, and keep you warm through all the dice rolling. Knit flat and focusing on intarsia these are a relatively simple introduction to colourwork.

Gauge

24 sts × 31 rows in stocking stitch

Yarn

GamerCrafting 100% Merino Dk
210 m/100 g in:

Lady Olenna's Poison (MC), 135 m/60 g
Coastal Kraken (CC), 40 m/20 g

Needles

3.25 mm/US 3 needles for working flat
3.5 mm/US 4 needles for working flat

Notions

Stitch holder or waste yarn
Needle for sewing up

Sizes

M[L] adult

Right mitt

CO 42[44] sts with smaller needles and MC.

Work 3.5 cm/1.5″ in a k1, p1 twisted rib. For twisted rib, knit through the back loop of every knit stitch, and purl every stitch as normal.

Switch to larger needles.

First row/set up row: K2, work the 20 st Right Tentacle chart using the intarsia method, pm, work the next 10 sts in the established twisted rib, pm, knit to end.

Next row: Purl to marker, sm, work the next 10 sts in the established twisted rib, sm, work row 2 of the chart, p2.

Row 1 (RS): K2, work the chart to the last stitch, k1fb, sm, work the next 10 sts in the established twisted rib, sm, k1fb, knit to end.

Row 2 (WS): Purl to marker, sm, work 10 sts in the established twisted rib, sm, purl to the first st of the chart, work the chart, p2.

Continue working each row in this manner, knitting on the right side and purling on the wrong side, making sure to keep the established twisted rib between the markers and creating increases on right side rows before the first marker and after the second. Do this until you have 60[64] sts total.

Once you have reached 60[64] sts on your needles:

Next row (RS): K2, work the chart, knit to marker. Remove marker, place 10 twisted rib sts onto a stitch holder or waste yarn. Remove second marker and knit to end of row. (50[54] sts on working needles, 10 sts on the stitch holder or waste yarn.)

Continue working as established, without increases, until the chart is completed.

Switch to smaller needles.

Work 2.5 cm/1″ in k1, p1 twisted rib.

Cast off with a stretchy cast off.

Thumb

Place the 10 sts from your waste yarn onto your left needle and backwards cast on 8[10] sts. Work in the established k1, p1 twisted rib for 5 rows.

Cast off with a stretchy cast off.

Seam the sides of the thumb together using mattress stitch. Sew the gap closed with the tail of the yarn.

Making up

Seam the sides of the mitt together using mattress stitch. Weave in ends, block.

Left mitt

First row/set up row: K10[12]sts, pm, work the next 10 sts in the established twisted rib, pm, work row 1 of the Left Tentacle chart, k2.

Next row: P2, work the second row of the chart, sm, work the next 10 sts in the established twisted rib, sm, purl to end.

Row 1: K9[11] sts, k1fb, sm, work the next 10 sts in the established twisted rib, k1fb in the first st of the chart, work the rest of the chart, k2.

Row 2: P2, work the next row of the chart, purl to marker, sm, work the next 10 sts in the established twisted rib, sm, purl to end.

Continue working each row in this manner, knitting on the right side and purling on the wrong side, making sure to keep the established twisted rib between the markers and creating increases on right side rows before the first marker and after the second. Do this until you have 60[64] sts total.

Once you have reached 60[64] sts on your needles:

Next row (RS): Knit to marker. Remove marker, place 10 twisted rib sts onto a stitch holder or waste yarn. Remove second marker and k to start of chart, work chart, k2.

Continue working as established, without increases, until the chart is completed.

Switch to smaller needles.

Work 2.5 cm/1″ in k1, p1 twisted rib.

Cast off with a stretchy cast off.

The thumb is worked in the same manner as the right mitt, and the making up instructions are the same.

Chart Right Tentacle

All RS rows are Knit rows, all WS rows are Purl rows.

Row 1 (RS): 3 MC, 10 CC, 7 MC. (20 sts)

Row 2 (WS): 7 MC, 4 CC, 4 MC, 2 CC, 3 MC.

Row 3: 2 MC, 2 CC, 1 MC, 4 CC, 1 MC, 3 CC, 7 MC.

Row 4: 7 MC, 3 CC, 1 MC, 4 CC, 1 MC, 2 CC, 2 MC.

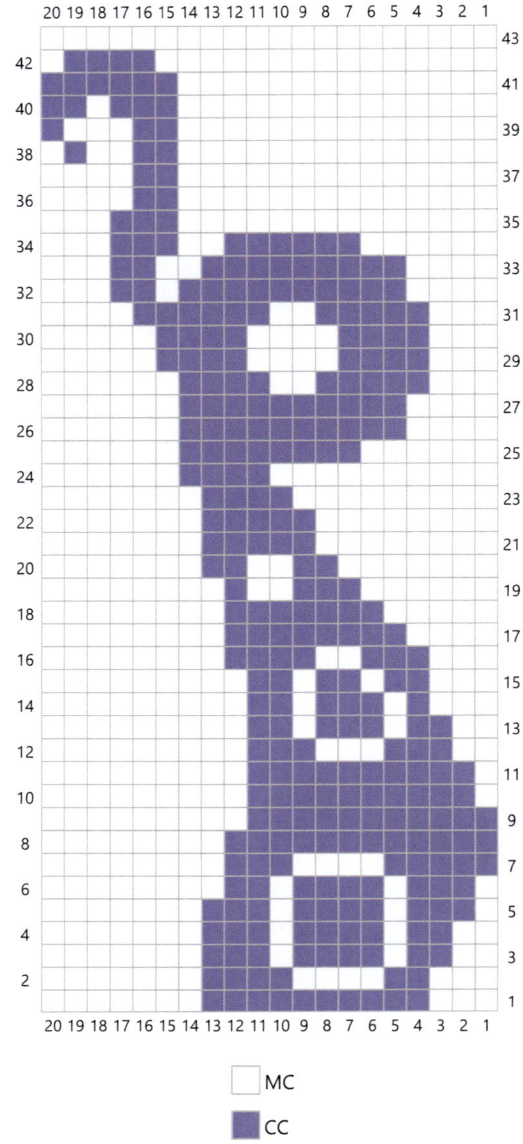

Right Tentacle chart

Row 5: 1 MC, 3 CC, 1 MC, 4 CC, 1 MC, 3 CC, 7 MC.

Row 6: 8 MC, 2 CC, 1 MC, 4 CC, 1 MC, 3 CC, 1 MC.

Row 7: 5 CC, 4 MC, 3 CC, 8 MC.

Row 8: 8 MC, 12 CC.

Row 9: 11 CC, 9 MC.

Row 10: 9 MC, 10 CC, 1 MC.

Row 11: 1 MC, 10 CC, 9 MC.

Row 12: 9 MC, 3 CC, 3 MC, 3 CC, 2 MC.

Row 13: 2 MC, 2 CC, 1 MC, 3 CC, 1 MC, 2 CC, 9 MC.

Row 14: 9 MC, 2 CC, 1 MC, 3 CC, 1 MC, 1 CC, 3 MC.

Row 15: 3 MC, (2 CC, 1 MC) × 2, 2 CC, 9 MC.

Row 16: 8 MC, 4 CC, 2 MC, 3 CC, 3 MC.

Row 17: 4 MC, 8 CC, 8 MC.

Row 18: 8 MC, 7 CC, 5 MC.

Row 19: 6 MC, 3 CC, 2 MC, 1 CC, 8 MC.

Row 20: 7 MC, 2 CC, 2 MC, 2 CC, 7 MC.

Row 21: 8 MC, 5 CC, 7 MC.

Row 22: 7 MC, 5 CC, 8 MC.

Row 23: 9 MC, 4 CC, 7 MC.

Row 24: 6 MC, 4 CC, 10 MC.

Row 25: 6 MC, 8 CC, 6 MC.

Row 26: 6 MC, 10 CC, 4 MC.

Row 27: 4 MC, 10 CC, 6 MC.

Row 28: 6 MC, 4 CC, 2 MC, 5 CC, 3 MC.

Row 29: 3 MC, 4 CC, 4 MC, 4 CC, 5 MC.

Row 30: 5 MC, 4 CC, 4 MC, 4 CC, 3 MC.

Row 31: 3 MC, 5 CC, 2 MC, 6 CC, 4 MC.

Row 32: 3 MC, 2 CC, 1 MC, 10 CC, 4 MC.

Row 33: 4 MC, 9 CC, 2 MC, 2 CC, 3 MC.

Row 34: 3 MC, 3 CC, 2 MC, 6 CC, 6 MC.

Row 35: 14 MC, 3 CC, 3 MC.

Row 36: 4 MC, 2 CC, 14 MC.

Row 37: 14 MC, 2 CC, 4 MC.

Row 38: 1 MC, 1 CC, 2 MC, 2 CC, 14 MC.

Row 39: 14 MC, 2 CC, 3 MC, 1 CC.

Row 40: 2 CC, 1 MC, 3 CC, 14 MC.

Row 41: 14 MC, 6 CC.

Row 42: 1 MC, 4 CC, 15 MC.

Row 43: Using MC, knit.

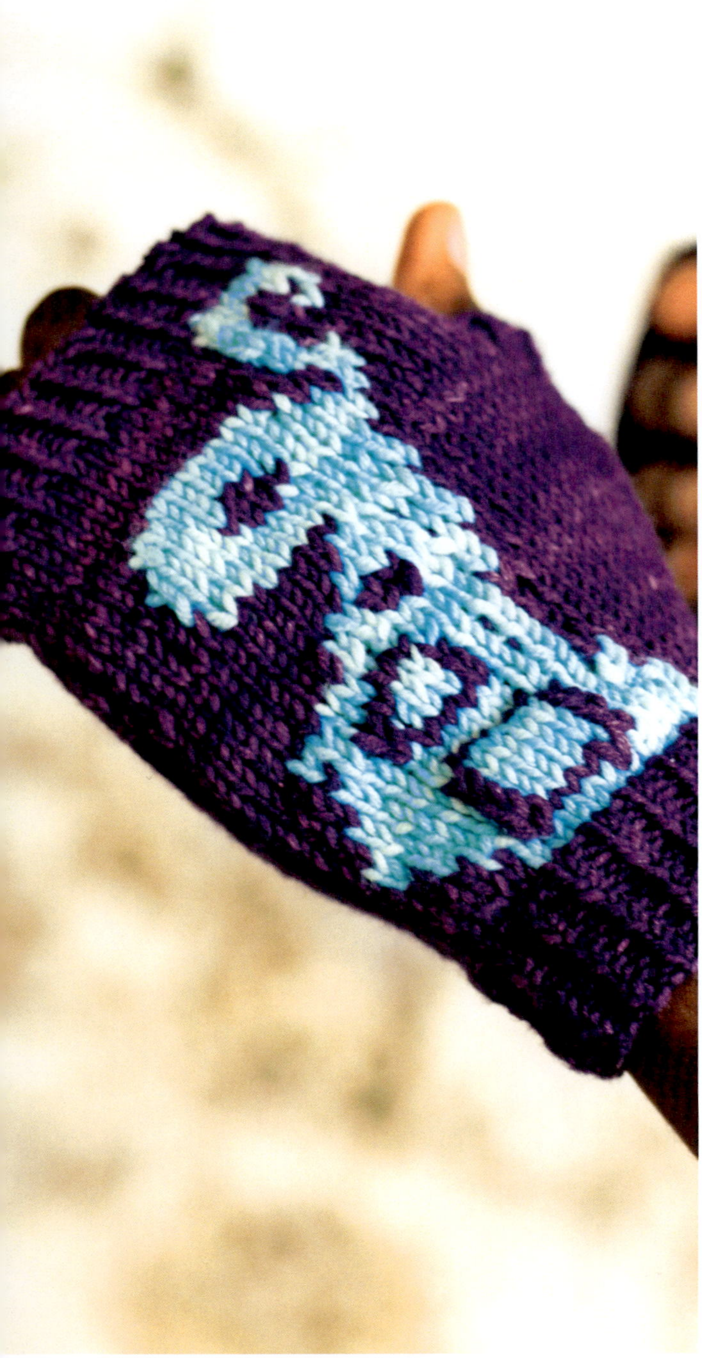

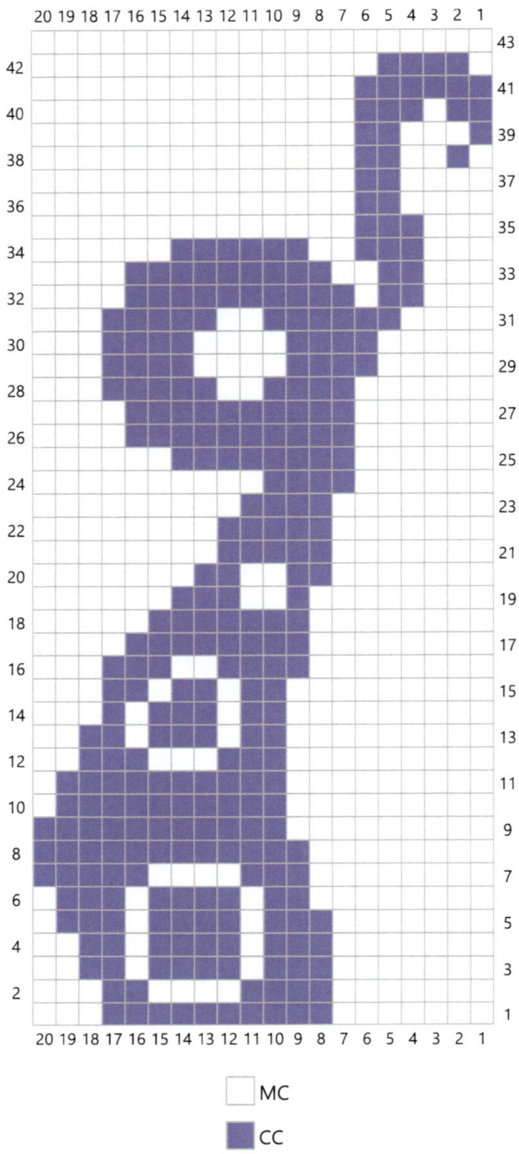

Left Tentacle chart

Chart Left Tentacle

All RS rows are Knit rows, all WS rows are Purl rows.

Row 1 (RS): 7 MC, 10 CC, 3 MC. (20 sts)

Row 2 (WS): 3 MC, 2 CC, 4 MC, 4 CC, 7 MC.

Row 3: 7 MC, 3 CC, 1 MC, 4 CC, 1 MC, 2 CC, 2 MC.

Row 4: 2 MC, 2 CC, 1 MC, 4 CC, 1 MC, 3 CC, 7 MC.

Row 5: 7 MC, 3 CC, 1 MC, 4 CC, 1 MC, 3 CC, 1 MC.

Row 6: 1 MC, 3 CC, 1 MC, 4 CC, 1 MC, 2 CC, 8 MC.

Row 7: 8 MC, 3 CC, 4 MC, 5 CC.

Row 8: 12 CC, 8 MC

Row 9: 9 MC, 11 CC.

Row 10: 1 MC, 10 CC, 9 MC.

Row 11: 9 MC, 10 CC, 1 MC.

Row 12: 2 MC, 3 CC, 3 MC, 3 CC, 9 MC.

Row 13: 9 MC, 2 CC, 1 MC, 3 CC, 1 MC, 2 CC, 2 MC.

Row 14: 3 MC, 1 CC, 1 MC, 3 CC, 1 MC, 2 CC, 9 MC.

Row 15: 9 MC, (2 CC, 1 MC) × 2, 2 CC, 3 MC.

Row 16: 3 MC, 3 CC, 2 MC, 4 CC, 8 MC.

Row 17: 8 MC, 8 CC, 4 MC.

Row 18: 5 MC, 7 CC, 8 MC.

Row 19: 8 MC, 1 CC, 2 MC, 3 CC, 6 MC.

Row 20: 7 MC, 2 CC, 2 MC, 2 CC, 7 MC.

Row 21: 7 MC, 5 CC, 8 MC.

Row 22: 8 MC, 5 CC, 7 MC.

Row 23: 7 MC, 4 CC, 9 MC.

Row 24: 10 MC, 4 CC, 6 MC.

Row 25: 6 MC, 8 CC, 6 MC.

Row 26: 4 MC, 10 CC, 6 MC.

Row 27: 6 MC, 10 CC, 4 MC.

Row 28: 3 MC, 5 CC, 2 MC, 4 CC, 6 MC.

Row 29: 5 MC, 4 CC, 4 MC, 4 CC, 3 MC.

Row 30: 3 MC, 4 CC, 4 MC, 4 CC, 5 MC.

Row 31: 4 MC, 6 CC, 2 MC, 5 CC, 3 MC.

Row 32: 4 MC, 10 CC, 1 MC, 2 CC, 3 MC.

Row 33: 3 MC, 2 CC, 2 MC, 9 CC, 4 MC.

Row 34: 6 MC, 6 CC, 2 MC, 3 CC, 3 MC.

Row 35: 3 MC, 3 CC, 14 MC.

Row 36: 14 MC, 2 CC, 4 MC.

Row 37: 4 MC, 2 CC, 14 MC.

Row 38: 14 MC, 2 CC, 2 MC, 1 CC, 1 MC.

Row 39: 1 CC, 3 MC, 2 CC, 14 MC.

Row 40: 14 MC, 3 CC, 1 MC, 2 CC.

Row 41: 6 CC, 14 MC.

Row 42: 15 MC, 4 CC, 1 MC.

Row 43: Using MC, knit.

Party Games

These games are characterised by their social aspect with direct interaction between the players, bringing in elements of fun and relaxation whilst also allowing for more light hearted games. The games we've picked here involve some of the most common party game mechanics: bluffing, co-operative building, and a blend of the two with competitive elements. The main focus in the patterns is visual simplicity, whilst playing with texture and colourwork to create some beautiful projects.

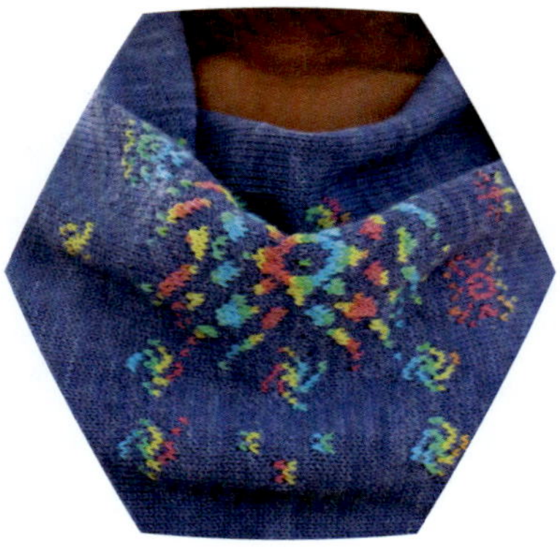

Chameleon Cowl

Helena Timms

This brightly coloured, textured knit cowl is perfect for standing out in a crowd and not being a chameleon! Based on the artwork from the box of the fun bluffing game of the same name, it uses linen stitch to blend the two colours together so they melt into each other and create some camouflage. This is a beginner knit using slip stitch stripes and ribbing in the round.

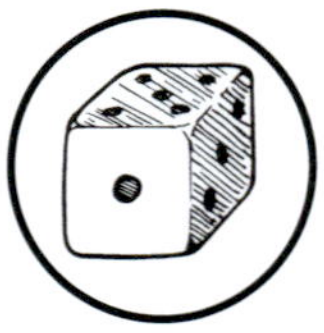

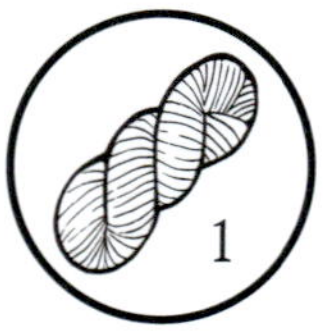

Yarn

John Arbon Textiles Yarnadelic in *English Sparrows* (MC) 333 m/100 g

2 × 25 g minis or 1 × 100 g skein of Sport weight

John Arbon Textiles Exmoor Sock yarn 4 ply in *Oddmedod* (CC) 400 m/100 g

1 × 50 g skein

This cowl can be made in any 4 ply or sport weight yarn – approx. 30–40 g needed for MC and 20–30 g for CC. Options given for additional width and depth would require more yarn.

Needles

3.25 mm/US 3 60 cm/24″ (or longer) circular needles for rib

3.75 mm/US 5 60 cm/24″ (or longer) circular needles for linen stitch

Notions

Stitch marker
Tapestry needle

Gauge

26 sts and 42 rounds in linen stitch pattern in 10 cm/4″ after blocking

Measurements

One size: 25 cm/10″ deep,
59 cm/23.25″ circumference

Options

For a wider slouchy cowl, cast on 200 stitches instead (78 cm/31″ circumference).

For a deeper cowl, continue in pattern until 5 cm/2″ shorter than desired or until CC runs out (but not MC!).

Begin

CO 152 sts using MC on smaller needles using long tail or stretchy method of your choice.

Join in the round being careful not to twist. Place marker to indicate start of round.

Work 10 rounds in 2 × 2 rib (k2, p2).

Body

Yarn is not broken for each colour change. When carrying yarn up the inside of the cowl between stripes, trap the hanging yarn with the working yarn to avoid gaps.

Switch to larger needles.

Knit 1 round.

Join CC and work linen stitch pattern.

Linen stitch pattern

Round 1 (CC): *K1, sl 1 wyif* to end.

Round 2 (CC): Knit to end.

Round 3 (MC): *Sl 1 wyif, k1* to end.

Round 4 (MC): Knit to end.

Work above 4 rounds 20 times total.

Break CC leaving a 15 cm/6″ tail for weaving in, and continue in MC.

End

Switch to smaller needles.

Work 10 rounds in 2 × 2 rib.

Cast off in rib pattern using your choice of stretchy method (I used a larger needle).

Weave in ends and wet block.

Hanabi Shawl

Diane Ugo

Hanabi is a game that requires intuition and great team work in order to produce a fireworks display that will be remembered for years to come. However, in this pattern, the stakes aren't so high. You can work the smaller fireworks as instructed or make up your own arrangement for a unique design.

However you choose to play with your colours, you'll have a display that is worthy of any night sky.

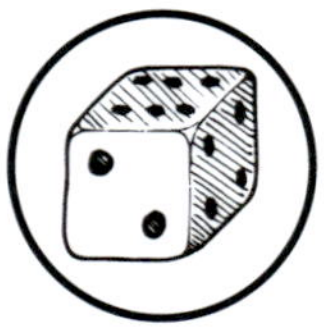

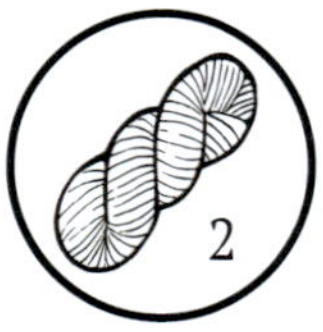

Yarn

Third Vault Yarns Companion 4ply in *Night Sky* (MC) 100% Superwash Merino 400 m/100 g, 2 skeins

Third Vault Yarns Companion sole in *Firework* (CC) 75% Superwash Merino 25% Nylon 20 m/5 g

Needles

3.5 mm/US 4 circular needles approx. 40 cm/16″

Notions

Stitch markers ×2
Tapestry needle

Gauge

30 sts × 40 rows to 10 cm/4″ in St st

Finished size

(Approx.) 167.5 cm/66″ (wingspan) × 49.5 cm/19.5″ (deep)

Pattern instructions

- The smaller fireworks leading up to the main display can be arranged according to the pattern instructions or you can design your own arrangement.
- Each chart states how many increases are produced when they are complete to help those working their own arrangement achieve the correct numbers of stitches for the main display (chart 9).
- At times it will be necessary to carry along the shade not in use, in order to have it available later in the row or in a different row. It is suggested to wrap the yarns every 4th or 5th stitch.
- Use stitch markers to indicate where each chart begins and ends.

Set-up

CO 3 sts.

Rows 1 & 2: Knit.

Row 3 (RS): K2, m1r, sl1wyif.

Row 4 (WS): K3, sl1wyif.

Row 5: K2, m1r, k1, sl1wyif.

Row 6 (and all WS rows): Knit to last st, sl1wyif.

Row 7: K2, m1r, k2, sl1wyif.

Row 9: K3, m1r, k2, sl1wyif.

Row 11: K3, m1r, k3, sl1wyif.

Row 12: Knit to last st, sl1wyif. (8 sts)

First half of shawl

Row 1 (RS): K4, yo, k3, sl1wyif. (9 sts)

Row 2 (WS): K4, p1, k3, sl1wyif.

Row 3: K4, yo, k to last sts, sl1wyif. (10 sts)

Row 4: K4, p to last 4 sts, k3, sl1wyif.

Repeat rows 3 & 4 until there are 61 sts (51 times).

Continue increases as established.

Row 107: Work, as set across 21 sts, pm, work from Chart 1, pm, work to end as set. (62 sts)

Row 108: Work as set to m, sm, work from Chart 1, sm, work to end as set.

Repeat until chart is worked in full, rm. (67 sts)

Rows 119–124: Work as set across 6 rows in MC. (70 sts)

Row 125: Work as set across 12 sts, pm, work from Chart 2, pm, work to end as set. (71 sts)

Row 126: Work as set to m, sm, work from Chart 2, sm, work to end as set.

Repeat until chart is worked in full, rm. (78 sts)

Rows 141–150: Work as set across 10 rows in MC. (83 sts)

Row 151: Work as set across 54 sts, pm, work from Chart 3, pm, work to end as set. (84 sts)

Row 152: Work as set to m, sm, work from Chart 3, sm, work to end as set.

Repeat until chart is worked in full, rm. (91 sts)

Rows 167–184: Work as set across 18 rows in MC. (100 sts)

Row 185: Work as set across 40 sts, pm, work from Chart 4, pm, work to end as set. (101 sts)

Row 186: Work as set to m, sm, work from Chart 4, sm, work to end as set.

Repeat until chart is worked in full, rm. (104 sts)

Rows 193 & 194: Work as set across 2 rows in MC. (105 sts)

Row 195: Work as set across 70 sts, pm, work from Chart 5, pm work to end as set. (106 sts)

Row 196: Work as set to m, sm, work from Chart 5, sm, work to end as set.

Repeat until chart is worked in full, rm. (111 sts)

Row 207: Work as set across 44 sts, pm, work from Chart 6, pm, work to end as set. (112 sts)

Row 208: Work as set to m, sm, work from Chart 6, sm, work to end as set.

Repeat until chart is worked in full, rm. (116 sts)

Row 217: Work as set across 26 sts, pm, work from Chart 4, pm, work to end as set. (117 sts)

Row 218: Work as set to m, sm, work from Chart 4, sm, work to end as set.

Repeat until chart is worked in full, rm. (120 sts)

Rows 225–228: Work as set across 4 rows in MC. (122 sts)

Row 229: Work as set across 76 sts, pm, work from Chart 7, pm, work to end as set. (123 sts)

Row 230: Work as set to m, sm, work from Chart 7, sm, work to end as set.

Repeat until chart is worked in full, rm. (127 sts)

Row 239: Work as set across 96 sts, pm, work from Chart 4, pm, work to end as set. (128 sts)

Row 240: Work as set to m, sm, work from Chart 4, sm, work to end as set.

Repeat until chart is worked in full, rm. (131 sts)

Rows 247–250: Work as set across 4 rows in MC. (133 sts)

Row 251: Work as set across 24 sts, pm, work from Chart 8, pm, work to end as set. (134 sts)

Row 252: Work as set to m, sm, work from Chart 8, sm, work to end as set.

Repeat until chart is worked in full, rm. (137 sts)

Main chart

Row 259: Work as set across 30 sts, pm, work first row of Chart 9, pm (after final st of chart), work as set to end. (138 sts)

Continue working from Chart 9, increasing on every RS row and working a sl1wyif at the end of each row.

After row 304 (row 46 of Chart 9, 160 sts), begin decreasing on every RS row as follows:

K4, yo, sl1kwise, k2tog, psso, k to last 4 sts, k3, sl1wyif.

Row 305 & all RS rows: K4, yo, sl1kwise, k2tog, psso, knit to m, sm, work from Chart 9, sm, work to last 4 sts, k3, sl1wyif. (159 sts)

Continue working WS rows as instructed.

There should be 136 sts when Chart 9 is complete.

Second half of shawl

Rows 353 & 354: Work as set in MC. (135 sts)

Row 355: Work as set across 95 sts, pm, work from Chart 8, pm, work to end as set. (134 sts)

Row 356: Work as set to m, sm, work from Chart 8, sm, work to end as set.

Repeat until chart is worked in full, rm. (131 sts)

Rows 363–366: Work as set across 4 rows in MC. (129 sts)

Row 367: Work as set across 23 sts, pm, work from Chart 4, pm, work to end as set. (128 sts)

Row 368: Work as set to m, sm, work from Chart 4, sm, work to end as set. (128 sts)

Repeat until chart is worked in full, rm. (125 sts)

Row 375: Work as set across 53 sts, pm, work from Chart 7, pm, work to end as set. (124 sts)

Row 376: Work as set to m, sm, work from Chart 7, sm, work to end as set.

Repeat until chart is worked in full, rm. (120 sts)

Rows 385–388: Work as set across 4 rows in MC. (118 sts)

Row 389: Work as set across 70 sts, pm, work from Chart 4, pm, work to end as set. (117 sts)

Row 390: Work as set to m, sm, work from Chart 4, sm, work to end as set.

Repeat until chart is worked in full, rm. (114 sts)

Row 397: Work as set across 23 sts, pm, work from Chart 6, pm, work to end as set. (113 sts)

Row 398: Work as set to m, sm, work from Chart 6, sm, work to end as set.

Repeat until chart is worked in full, rm. (109 sts)

Row 407: Work as set across 49 sts, pm, work from Chart 5, pm, work to end as set. (108 sts)

Row 408: Work as set to m, sm, work from Chart 5, sm, work to end as set.

Repeat until chart is worked in full, rm. (103 sts)

Rows 419–422: Work as set across 4 rows in MC. (101 sts)

Row 423: Work as set across 60 sts, pm, work from Chart 4, pm, work to end as set. (100 sts)

Row 424: Work as set to m, sm, work from Chart 4, sm, work to end as set.

Repeat until chart is worked in full, rm. (97 sts)

Rows 431–448: Work as set across 18 rows in MC. (88 sts)

Row 449: Work as set across 18 sts, pm, work from Chart 10, pm, work to end as set. (87 sts)

Row 450: Work as set to m, sm, work from Chart 10, sm, work to end as set.

Repeat until chart is worked in full, rm. (82 sts)

Rows 461–474: Work as set across 14 rows in MC. (75 sts)

Row 475: Work as set across 46 sts, pm, work from Chart 2, pm, work to end as set. (74 sts)

Row 476: Work as set to m, sm, work from Chart 2, sm, work to end as set.

Repeat until chart is worked in full, rm. (67 sts)

Rows 491–474: Work as set in MC only until 10 sts remain.

End

Row 1: K3, k2tog, knit to last st, sl1wyif. (9 sts)

Row 2 and all WS rows: knit to the last st, sl1wyif.

Row 3: Repeat row 1. (8 sts)

Row 5: K2, k2tog, knit to last st, sl1wyif. (7 sts)

Repeat row 5 (on RS) until 5 sts remain.

Row 11: K1, k2tog, k1, sl1wyif. (4 sts)

Row 13: K1, k2tog, sl1wyif. (3 sts)

Rows 14–16: Knit.

BO last 3 sts.

Sew in ends and block.

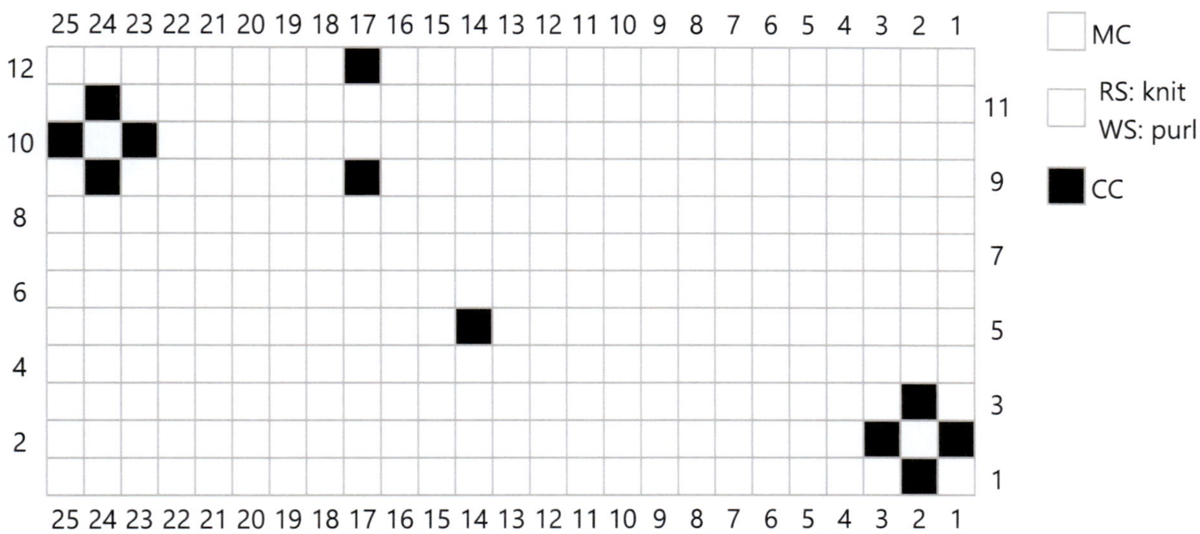

Chart 1: 6 stitches increased.

Charts

When knitting from the charts, please note that all RS rows are Knit rows and all WS rows are Purl rows.

Chart 1

This chart is worked over 25 sts.

Row 1 (RS): 1 MC, 1 CC, 23 MC.

Row 2 (WS): 22 MC, 1 CC, 1 MC, 1 CC.

Row 3: Repeat row 1.

Row 4: Using MC, purl.

Row 5: 13 MC, 1 CC, 11 MC.

Row 6: Using MC, purl.

Row 7: Using MC, knit.

Row 8: Using MC, purl.

Row 9: 16 MC, 1 CC, 6 MC, 1 CC, 1 MC.

Row 10: 1 CC, 1 MC, 1 CC, 22 MC.

Row 11: 23 MC, 1 CC, 1 MC.

Row 12: 8 MC, 1 CC, 16 MC.

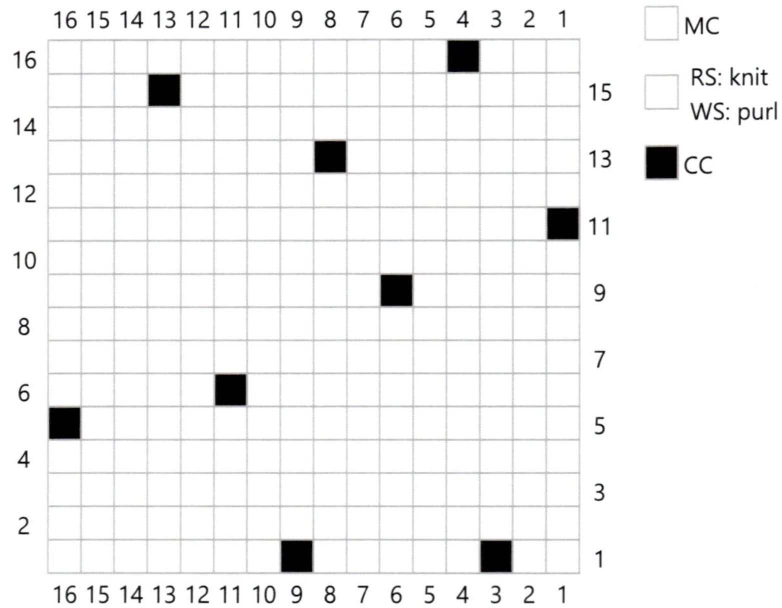

Chart 2: 8 stitches increased.

Chart 2

This chart is worked over 16 sts.

Row 1 (RS): 2 MC, 1 CC, 5 MC, 1 CC, 7 MC.

Row 2 (WS): Using MC, purl.

Row 3: Using MC, knit.

Row 4: Using MC, purl.

Row 5: 15 MC, 1 CC.

Row 6: 5 MC, 1 CC, 10 MC.

Row 7: Using MC, knit.

Row 8: Using MC, purl.

Row 9: 5 MC, 1 CC, 10 MC.

Row 10: Using MC, purl.

Row 11: 1 CC, 15 MC.

Row 12: Using MC, purl.

Row 13: 7 MC, 1 CC, 8 MC.

Row 14: Using MC, purl.

Row 15: 12 MC, 1 CC, 3 MC.

Row 16: 12 MC, 1 CC, 3 MC.

Chart 3

This chart is worked over 19 sts.

Row 1 (RS): 7 MC, 1 CC, 11 MC. (19 sts)

Row 2 (WS): 7 MC, 1 CC, 11 MC.

Row 3: Using MC, knit.

Row 4: 9 MC, 1 CC, 6 MC, 1 CC, 2 MC.

Row 5: 1 CC, 3 MC, 1 CC, 14 MC.

Row 6: 4 MC, 1 CC, 6 MC, 1 CC, 7 MC.

Row 7: 3 MC, (1 CC, 6 MC) × 2, 1 CC, 1 MC.

Row 8: Using MC, purl.

Row 9: Using MC, knit.

Row 10: 1 CC, 3 MC, 1 CC, 5 MC, 1 CC, 7 MC, 1 CC.

Row 11: 3 MC, 1 CC, 15 MC.

Row 12: Using MC, purl.

Row 13: 6 MC, 1 CC, 2 MC, 1 CC, 3 MC, 1 CC, 5 MC.

Row 14: Using MC, purl.

Row 15: 17 MC, 1 CC, 1 MC.

Row 16: Using MC, purl.

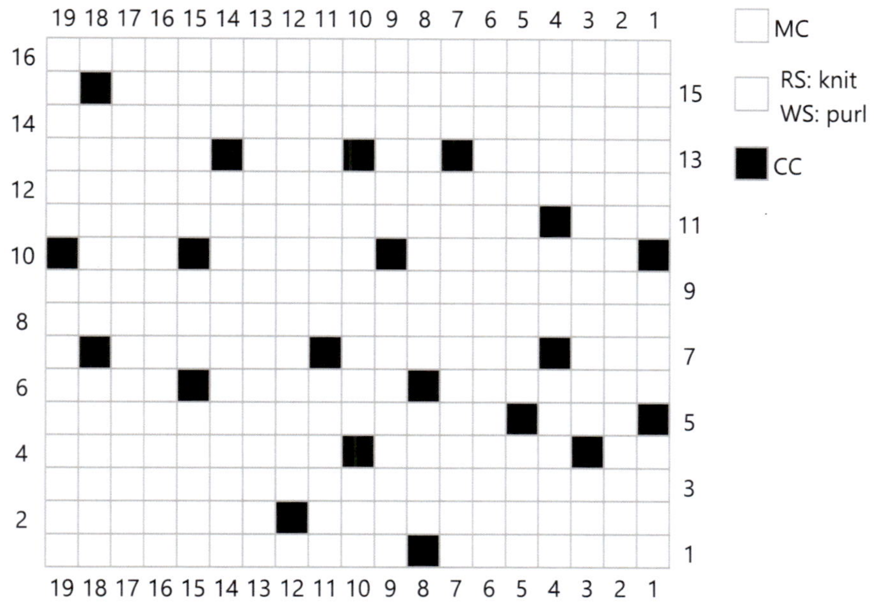

Chart 3: 8 stitches increased.

Chart 4

This chart is worked over 7 sts.

Row 1 (RS): 4 MC, 1 CC, 2 MC.

Row 2 (WS): 1 MC, 1 CC, 2 MC, 2 CC, 1 MC.

Row 3: 1 CC, 2 MC, (1 CC, 1 MC) × 2.

Row 4: 2 MC, 3 CC, 2 MC.

Row 5: (1 MC, 1 CC) × 2, 2 MC, 1 CC.

Row 6: 1 MC, 2 CC, 2 MC, 1 CC, 1 MC.

Row 7: 2 MC, 1 CC, 4 MC.

Row 8: Using MC, purl.

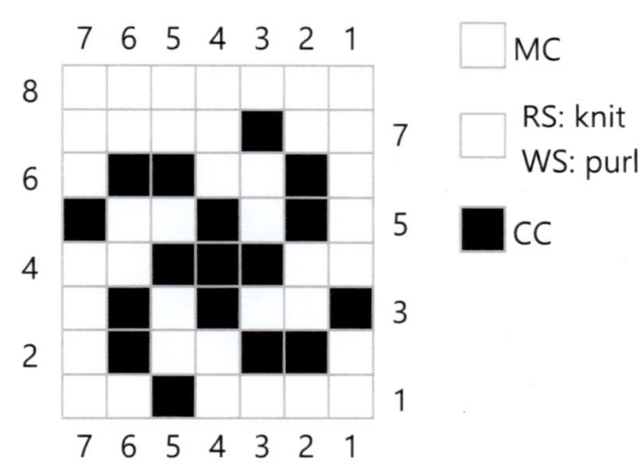

Chart 4: 8 stitches increased.

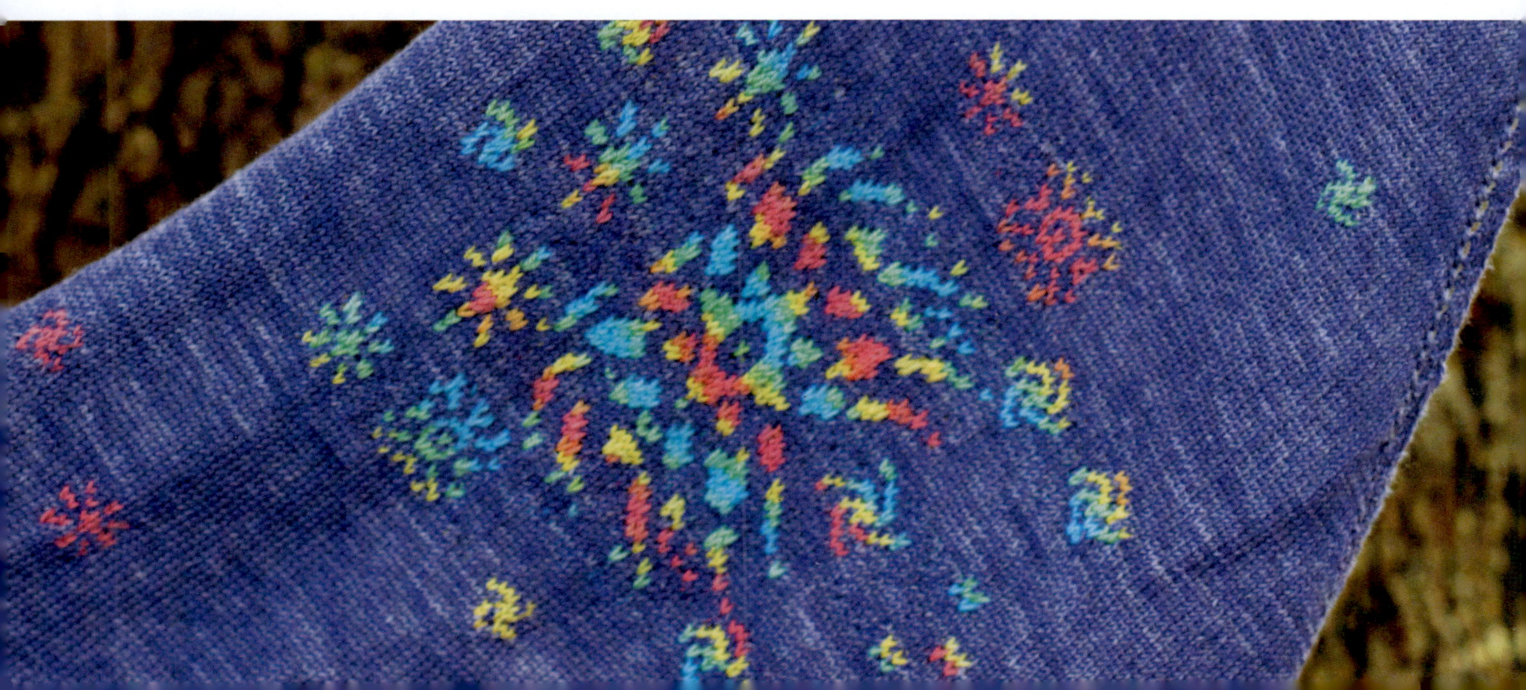

Chart 5

This chart is worked over 14 sts.

Row 1 (RS): 1 CC, 3 MC, 1 CC, 7 MC, 1 CC, 1 MC. (14 sts)

Row 2 (WS): Using MC, purl.

Row 3: Using MC, knit.

Row 4: (1 CC, 6 MC) × 2.

Row 5: 3 MC, 1 CC, 5 MC, 1 CC, 4 MC.

Row 6: Using MC, purl.

Row 7: 6 MC, 1 CC, 7 MC.

Row 8: Using MC, purl.

Row 9: Using MC, knit.

Row 10: Using MC, purl.

Row 11: (5 MC, 1 CC) × 2, 2 MC.

Row 12: Using MC, purl.

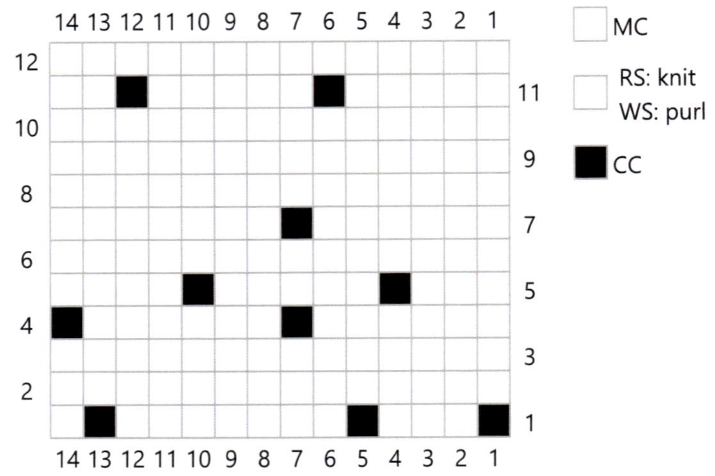

Chart 5: 6 stitches increased.

Chart 6

This chart is worked over 10 sts.

Row 1 (RS): 2 MC, 1 CC, 4 MC, 1 CC, 2 MC.

Row 2 (WS): Using MC, purl.

Row 3: Using MC, knit.

Row 4: Using MC, purl.

Row 5: 9 MC, 1 CC.

Row 6: Using MC, purl.

Row 7: 3 MC, 1 CC, 6 MC.

Row 8: Using MC, purl.

Row 9: 1 CC, 9 MC.

Row 10: 4 MC, 1 CC, 5 MC.

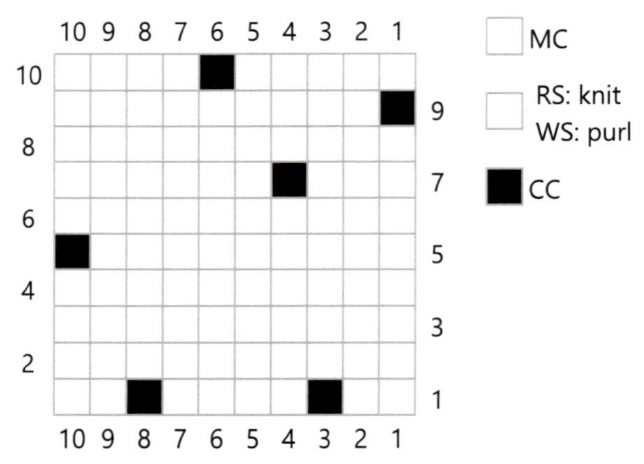

Chart 6: 5 stitches increased.

Chart 7

This chart is worked over 9 sts.

Row 1 (RS): 4 MC, 1 CC, 4 MC.

Row 2 (WS): 1 MC, (1 CC, 2 MC) × 2, 1 CC, 1 MC.

Row 3: 2 MC, 1 CC, 3 MC, 1 CC, 2 MC.

Row 4: 4 MC, 1 CC, 4 MC.

Row 5: 2 CC, 1 MC, 3 CC, 1 MC, 2 CC.

Row 6: repeat row 4.

Row 7: repeat row 3.

Row 8: repeat row 2.

Row 9: repeat row 1.

Row 10: Using MC, purl.

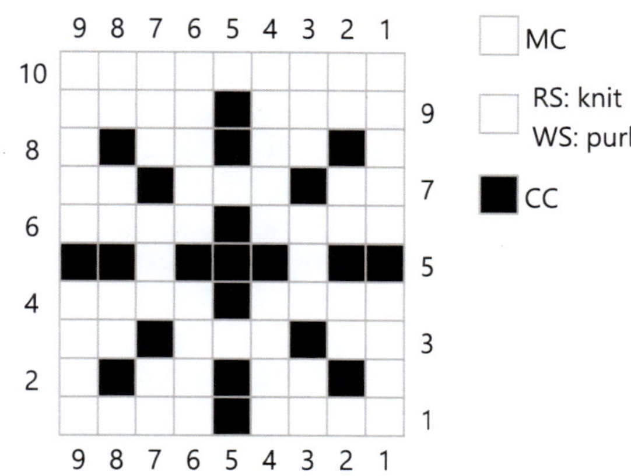

Chart 7: 5 stitches increased.

Chart 8

This chart is worked over 10 sts.

Row 1 (RS): 1 CC, 2 MC, 1 CC, 4 MC, 1 CC, 1 MC.

Row 2 (WS): Using MC, purl.

Row 3: Using MC, knit.

Row 4: 3 MC, 1 CC, 6 MC.

Row 5: 3 MC, 1 CC, 6 MC.

Row 6: 9 MC, 1 CC.

Row 7: 2 MC, 1 CC, 4 MC, 1 CC, 2 MC.

Row 8: 1 CC, 9 MC.

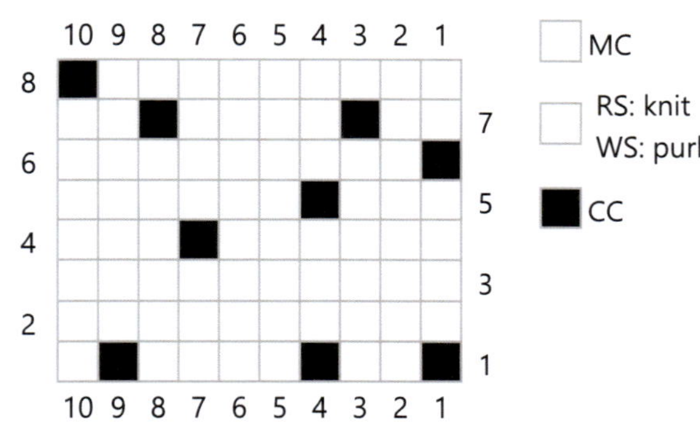

Chart 8: 4 stitches increased.

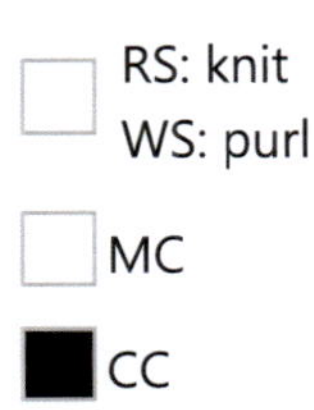

Key for Chart 9 (over page).

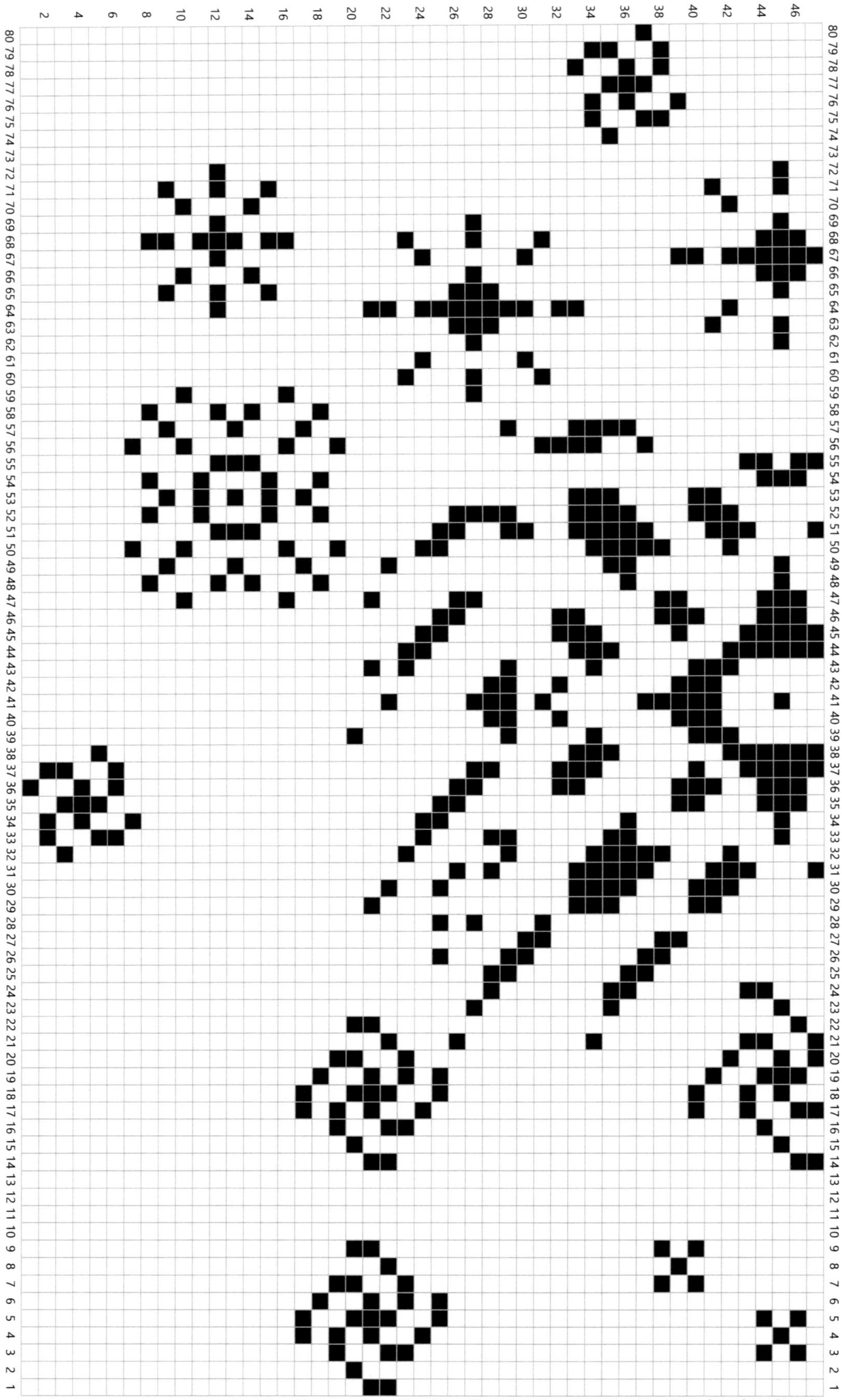

Chart 9, part 1.

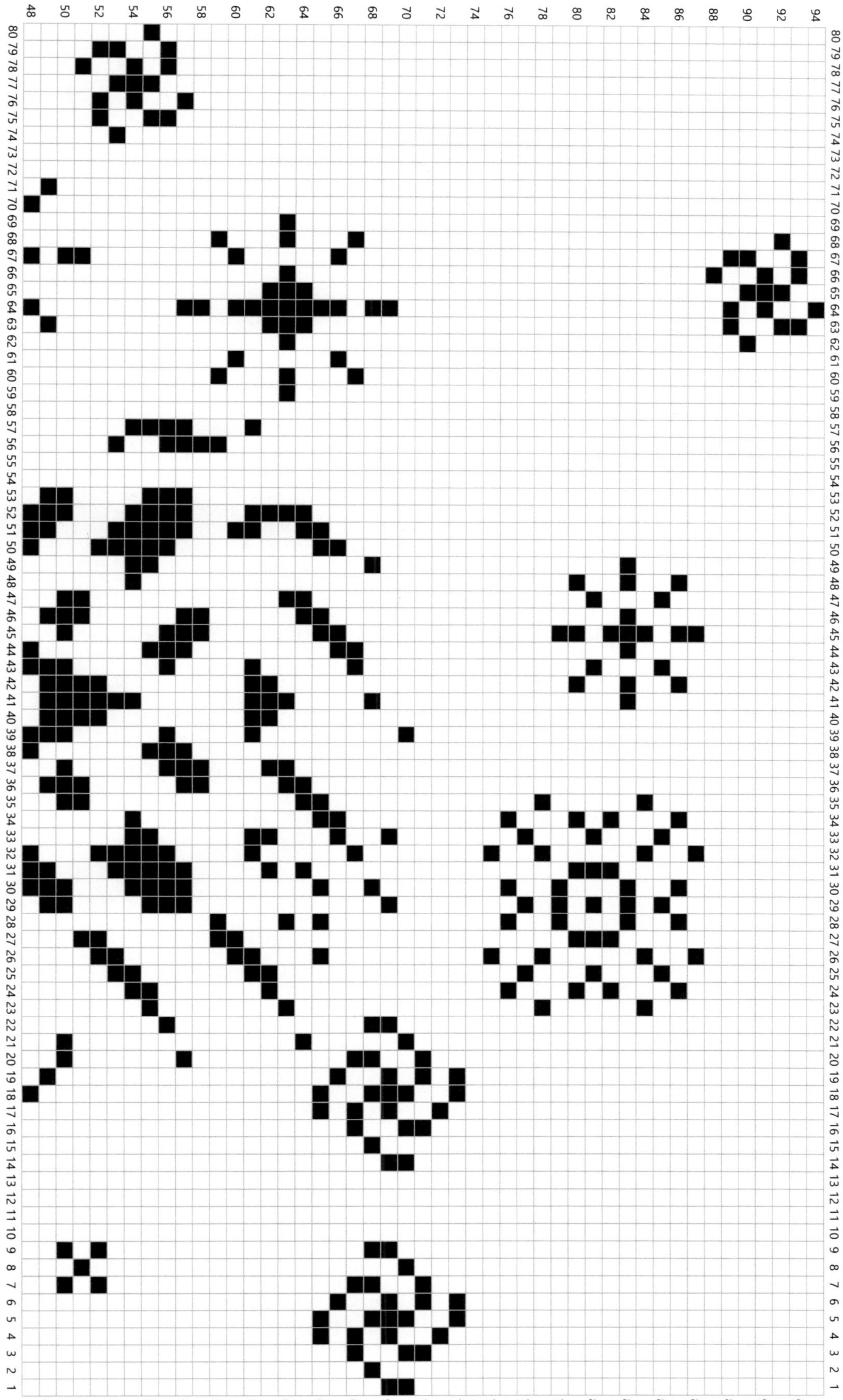

Chart 9, part 2.

Chart 9

This chart is worked over 80 sts.

Row 1 (RS): 35 MC, 1 CC, 44 MC.

Row 2 (WS): 43 MC, 1 CC, 2 MC, 2 CC, 32 MC.

Row 3: 31 MC, 1 CC, 2 MC, 1 CC, 1 MC, 1 CC, 43 MC.

Row 4: 44 MC, 3 CC, 33 MC.

Row 5: 32 MC, 1 CC, 1 MC, 1 CC, 2 MC, 1 CC, 42 MC.

Row 6: 43 MC, 2 CC, 2 MC, 1 CC, 32 MC.

Row 7: 33 MC, 1 CC, 15 MC, 1 CC, 5 MC, 1 CC, 24 MC.

Row 8: 8 MC, 4 MC, 1 CC, 4 MC, 5 MC, 1 CC, 3 MC, 1 CC, 1 MC, 1 CC, 3 MC, 1 CC, 47 MC.

Row 9: 48 MC, (1 CC, 3 MC) × 2, 1 CC, 6 MC, 1 MC, (1 CC, 2 MC) × 2, 1 CC, 1 MC, 8 MC.

Row 10: 8 MC, 2 MC, 1 CC, 3 MC, 1 CC, 2 MC, 4 MC, 1 CC, 2 MC, 1 CC, 5 MC, 1 CC, 2 MC, 1 CC, 46 MC.

Row 11: 51 MC, 3 CC, 9 MC, 4 MC, 1 CC, 4 MC, 8 MC.

Row 12: 8 MC, 2 CC, 1 MC, 3 CC, 1 MC, 2 CC, 5 MC, 1 CC, 2 MC, 1 CC, 3 MC, 1 CC, 2 MC, 1 CC, 47 MC.

Row 13: 48 MC, (1 CC, 1 MC) × 4, 1 CC, 6 MC, 4 MC, 1 CC, 4 MC, 8 MC.

Row 14: 8 MC, 2 MC, 1 CC, 3 MC, 1 CC, 2 MC, 5 MC, 1 CC, 2 MC, 1 CC, 3 MC, 1 CC, 2 MC, 1 CC, 47 MC.

Row 15: 51 MC, 3 CC, 9 MC, 1 MC, (1 CC, 2 MC) × 2, 1 CC, 1 MC, 8 MC.

Row 16: 8 MC, 4 MC, 1 CC, 4 MC, 4 MC, 1 CC, 2 MC, 1 CC, 5 MC, 1 CC, 2 MC, 1 CC, 46 MC.

Row 17: 3 MC, 2 CC, 11 MC, 2 CC, 30 MC, (1 CC, 3 MC) × 2, 1 CC, 23 MC.

Row 18: 22 MC, 1 CC, 3 MC, 1 CC, 1 MC, 1 CC, 3 MC, 1 CC, 28 MC, 1 CC, 12 MC, 1 CC, 5 MC.

Row 19: 2 MC, 2 CC, 2 MC, 1 CC, 8 MC, 2 CC, 2 MC, 1 CC, 29 MC, 1 CC, 5 MC, 1 CC, 24 MC.

Row 20: 41 MC, 1 CC, 16 MC, (1 CC, 1 MC) × 2, 1 CC, 2 MC, 1 CC, 5 MC, (1 CC, 1 MC) × 2, 1 CC, 2 MC, 1 CC, 1 MC.

Row 21: 1 CC, 2 MC, 3 CC, 2 MC, 1 CC, 4 MC, 1 CC, 2 MC, 3 CC, 2 MC, 1 CC, 6 MC, 1 CC, 13 MC, 1 CC, 3 MC, (1 CC, 16 MC) × 2.

Row 22: 16 MC, 1 CC, 14 MC, 1 CC, 7 MC, 1 CC, 10 MC, 1 CC, 8 MC, 1 CC, 2 MC, (1 CC, 1 MC) × 2, 1 CC, 5 MC, 1 CC, 2 MC, (1 CC, 1 MC) × 2, 1 CC.

Row 23: 2 MC, 1 CC, 2 MC, 2 CC, 8 MC, 1 CC, 2 MC, 2 CC, 11 MC, 1 CC, 10 MC, 2 CC, 15 MC, 1 CC, 7 MC, 1 CC, 12 MC.

Row 24: 13 MC, (1 CC, 2 MC) × 2, 1 CC, 10 MC, 1 CC, 4 MC, 2 CC, 9 MC, 2 CC, 15 MC, 1 CC, 12 MC, 1 CC, 3 MC.

Row 25: 4 MC, 2 CC, 11 MC, 2 CC, 6 MC, (1 CC, 1 MC) × 2, 1 CC, 3 MC, 2 CC, 9 MC, 2 CC, 3 MC, 2 CC, 12 MC, 1 CC, 16 MC.

Row 26: 15 MC, 3 CC, 10 MC, 2 CC, 3 MC, 2 CC, 9 MC, 2 CC, 3 MC, 1 CC, 9 MC, 1 CC, 20 MC.

Row 27: 22 MC, 1 CC, 4 MC, 1 CC, 7 MC, 2 CC, 3 MC, 1 CC, 5 MC, 1 CC, 4 MC, 1 CC, 6 MC, 2 CC, 1 MC, 5 CC, 1 MC, 2 CC, 11 MC.

Row 28: 15 MC, 3 CC, 10 MC, 1 CC, 9 MC, 3 CC, 2 MC, 1 CC, 3 MC, 1 CC, 1 MC, 1 CC, 5 MC, 2 CC, 23 MC.

Row 29: 24 MC, (2 CC, 5 MC) × 2, 5 CC, 7 MC, 2 CC, 4 MC, 1 CC, 6 MC, 1 CC, 16 MC.

Row 30: 13 MC, (1 CC, 2 MC) × 2, 1 CC, 9 MC, 1 CC, 23 MC, 2 CC, 25 MC.

Row 31: 26 MC, 2 CC, 12 MC, 1 CC, 14 MC, 1 CC, 3 MC, 1 CC, 7 MC, 1 CC, 12 MC.

Row 32: 16 MC, 1 CC, 7 MC, 1 CC, 9 MC, 2 CC, 2 MC, 1 CC, 1 MC, 1 CC, 2 MC, 2 CC, 35 MC.

Row 33: 28 MC, 3 CC, 4 MC, 3 CC, 5 MC, 3 CC, 4 MC, 3 CC, 2 MC, 2 CC, 6 MC, 1 CC, 13 MC, 1 CC, 2 MC.

Row 34: 1 MC, 1 CC, 2 MC, 2 CC, 17 MC, 2 CC, 2 MC, 4 CC, 4 MC, 3 CC, 3 MC, 3 CC, 4 MC, 4 CC, 7 MC, 1 CC, 20 MC.

Row 35: 22 MC, 2 CC, 4 MC, 5 CC, 4 MC, 1 CC, 5 MC, 1 CC, 4 MC, 5 CC, 3 MC, 1 CC, 16 MC, 1 CC, 2 MC, (1 CC, 1 MC) × 2.

Row 36: 2 MC, 3 CC, 18 MC, 1 CC, 4 MC, 5 CC, 13 MC, 5 CC, 4 MC, 2 CC, 23 MC.

Row 37: 24 MC, 2 CC, 4 MC, 2 CC, 8 MC, 1 CC, 8 MC, 2 CC, 4 MC, 1 CC, 18 MC, 1 CC, 1 MC, 1 CC, 2 MC, 1 CC.

Row 38: 1 MC, 2 CC, 2 MC, 1 CC, 24 MC, 1 CC, 2 MC, 2 CC, 4 MC, 1 CC, 8 MC, 1 CC, 4 MC, 2 CC, 16 MC, 1 CC, 1 MC, 1 CC, 6 MC.

Row 39: 7 MC, 1 CC, 18 MC, 1 CC, 7 MC, 2 CC, 3 MC, 3 CC, 2 MC, 3 CC, 19 MC, 1 CC, 8 MC, 1 CC, 4 MC.

Row 40: 13 MC, 1 CC, 13 MC, 2 CC, 5 MC, 1 CC, 2 MC, 5 CC, 1 MC, 3 CC, 4 MC, 2 CC, 10 MC, 2 CC, 7 MC, 1 CC, 1 MC, 1 CC, 6 MC.

Row 41: 18 MC, 1 CC, 9 MC, 3 CC, 4 MC, 1 CC, 2 MC, 5 CC, 7 MC, 3 CC, 9 MC, 1 CC, 7 MC, 1 CC, 9 MC.

Row 42: 10 MC, (1 CC, 2 MC) × 2, 1 CC, 11 MC, 3 CC, 5 MC, 2 CC, 3 MC, 2 CC, 5 MC, 3 CC, 9 MC, 1 CC, 19 MC.

Row 43: 16 MC, 2 CC, (2 MC, 1 CC) × 2, 6 MC, 1 CC, (5 MC, 2 CC) × 2, 5 MC, 1 CC, 3 MC, 1 CC, 11 MC, 1 CC, 13 MC.

Row 44: 12 MC, 3 CC, 10 MC, 2 CC, 6 MC, 4 CC, 5 MC, 4 CC, 10 MC, 1 CC, 2 MC, 1 CC, 1 MC, 1 CC, 2 MC, 1 CC, 10 MC, 1 CC, 1 MC, 1 CC, 2 MC.

Row 45: 3 MC, 1 CC, 10 MC, 1 CC, 2 MC, 3 CC, 2 MC, 1 CC, 9 MC, 6 CC, 2 MC, 1 CC, 2 MC, 6 CC, 4 MC, 1 CC, 7 MC, 2 CC, 1 MC, 5 CC, 1 MC, 2 CC, 8 MC.

Row 46: 12 MC, 3 CC, 10 MC, 2 CC, 6 MC, 4 CC, 5 MC, 4 CC, 12 MC, 1 CC, 2 MC, 1 CC, 1 MC, 1 CC, 2 MC, 1 CC, 8 MC, 1 CC, 1 MC, 1 CC, 2 MC.

Row 47: 13 MC, (1 CC, 2 MC) × 2, 2 CC, 9 MC, 1 CC, (5 MC, 2 CC) × 2, 5 MC, 1 CC, 3 MC, 1 CC, 11 MC, 1 CC, 13 MC.

Row 48: 10 MC, (1 CC, 2 MC) × 2, 1 CC, 11 MC, 3 CC, 5 MC, 2 CC, 3 MC, 2 CC, 5 MC, 3 CC, 11 MC, 1 CC, 17 MC.

Row 49: 18 MC, 1 CC, 9 MC, 3 CC, 4 MC, 1 CC, 2 MC, 5 CC, 2 MC, 1 CC, 4 MC, 3 CC, 9 MC, 1 CC, 7 MC, 1 CC, 9 MC.

Row 50: 13 MC, 1 CC, 13 MC, 2 CC, 4 MC, 3 CC, 1 MC, 5 CC, 1 MC, 3 CC, 4 MC, 2 CC, 7 MC, 2 CC, 10 MC, 1 CC, 1 MC, 1 CC, 6 MC.

Row 51: 7 MC, 1 CC, 18 MC, 1 CC, 7 MC, 2 CC, 3 MC, 3 CC, 3 MC, 2 CC, 19 MC, 1 CC, 10 MC, 1 CC, 2 MC.

Row 52: 1 MC, 1 CC, 2 MC, 2 CC, 24 MC, 1 CC, 7 MC, 3 CC, 7 MC, 1 CC, 4 MC, 2 CC, 16 MC, 1 CC, 1 MC, 1 CC, 6 MC.

Row 53: 24 MC, 2 CC, 4 MC, 2 CC, 8 MC, 1 CC, 8 MC, 2 CC, 4 MC, 1 CC, 17 MC, 1 CC, 2 MC, (1 CC, 1 MC) × 2.

Row 54: 2 MC, 3 CC, 18 MC, 1 CC, 4 MC, 5 CC, 6 MC, 1 CC, 6 MC, 5 CC, 4 MC, 2 CC, 23 MC.

Row 55: 22 MC, 2 CC, 4 MC, 5 CC, 4 MC, 1 CC, 5 MC, 1 CC, 4 MC, 5 CC, 3 MC, 1 CC, 17 MC, 1 CC, 1 MC, 1 CC, 2 MC, 1 CC.

Row 56: 1 MC, 2 CC, 2 MC, 1 CC, 17 MC, 2 CC, 2 MC, 4 CC, 4 MC, 3 CC, 3 MC, 3 CC, 4 MC, 4 CC, 6 MC, 1 CC, 21 MC.

Row 57: 19 MC, 1 CC, 8 MC, 3 CC, 4 MC, 3 CC, 5 MC, 3 CC, 4 MC, 3 CC, 2 MC, 2 CC, 6 MC, 1 CC, 11 MC, 1 CC, 4 MC.

Row 58: 16 MC, 1 CC, 7 MC, 1 CC, 9 MC, 2 CC, 7 MC, 2 CC, 35 MC.

Row 59: 26 MC, 2 CC, 27 MC, 1 CC, 3 MC, 1 CC, 7 MC, 1 CC, 12 MC.

Row 60: repeat row 30.

Row 61: repeat row 29.

Row 62: repeat row 28.

Row 63: repeat row 27.

Row 64: repeat row 26.

Row 65: 3 MC, 2 CC, 11 MC, 2 CC, 7 MC, (1 CC, 1 MC) × 2, 1 CC, 3 MC, 2 CC, 9 MC, 2 CC, 3 MC, 2 CC, 12 MC, 1 CC, 16 MC.

Row 66: 13 MC, (1 CC, 2 MC) × 2, 1 CC, 10 MC, 1 CC, 4 MC, 2 CC, 9 MC, 2 CC, 13 MC, 1 CC, 12 MC, 1 CC, 5 MC.

Row 67: 2 MC, 2 CC, 2 MC, 1 CC, 8 MC, 2 CC, 2 MC, 1 CC, 11 MC, 1 CC, 10 MC, 2 CC, 15 MC, 1 CC, 7 MC, 1 CC, 12 MC.

Row 68: 16 MC, 1 CC, 14 MC, 1 CC, 7 MC, 1 CC, 10 MC, 1 CC, 7 MC, (1 CC, 1 MC) × 2, 1 CC, 2 MC, 1 CC, 5 MC, (1 CC, 1 MC) × 2, 1 CC, 2 MC, 1 CC, 1 MC.

Row 69: 1 CC, 2 MC, 3 CC, 2 MC, 1 CC, 4 MC, 1 CC, 2 MC, 3 CC, 2 MC, 1 CC, 6 MC, 1 CC, 3 MC, 1 CC, 30 MC, 1 CC, 16 MC.

Row 70: 41 MC, 1 CC, 17 MC, 1 CC, 2 MC, (1 CC, 1 MC) × 2, 1 CC, 5 MC, 1 CC, 2 MC, (1 CC, 1 MC) × 2, 1 CC.

Row 71: 2 MC, 1 CC, 2 MC, 2 CC, 8 MC, 1 CC, 2 MC, 2 CC, 60 MC.

Row 72: 63 MC, 1 CC, 12 MC, 1 CC, 3 MC.

Row 73: 4 MC, 2 CC, 11 MC, 2 CC, 61 MC.

Row 74: Using MC, purl.

Row 75: 25 MC, 1 CC, 5 MC, 1 CC, 48 MC.

Row 76: 46 MC, 1 CC, 3 MC, 1 CC, 1 MC, 1 CC, 3 MC, 1 CC, 23 MC.

Row 77: 24 MC, (1 CC, 3 MC) × 2, 1 CC, 47 MC.

Row 78: 45 MC, 1 CC, 2 MC, 1 CC, 5 MC, 1 CC, 2 MC, 1 CC, 22 MC.

Row 79: 27 MC, 3 CC, 10 MC, 4 MC, 1 CC, 4 MC, 31 MC.

Row 80: 31 MC, 1 MC, (1 CC, 2 MC) × 2, 1 CC, 1 MC, 6 MC, 1 CC, 2 MC, 1 CC, 3 MC, 1 CC, 2 MC, 1 CC, 23 MC.

Row 81: 24 MC, (1 CC, 1 MC) × 4, 1 CC, 7 MC, 2 MC, 1 CC, 3 MC, 1 CC, 2 MC, 31 MC.

Row 82: 31 MC, 4 MC, 1 CC, 4 MC, 6 MC, 1 CC, 2 MC, 1 CC, 3 MC, 1 CC, 2 MC, 1 CC, 23 MC.

Row 83: 27 MC, 3 CC, 10 MC, 2 CC, 1 MC, 3 CC, 1 MC, 2 CC, 31 MC.

Row 84: 31 MC, 4 MC, 1 CC, 4 MC, (5 MC, 1 CC, 2 MC, 1 CC) × 2, 22 MC.

Row 85: 24 MC, (1 CC, 3 MC) × 2, 1 CC, 7 MC, 2 MC, 1 CC, 3 MC, 1 CC, 2 MC, 31 MC.

Row 86: 31 MC, 1 MC, (1 CC, 2 MC) × 2, 1 CC, 1 MC, 6 MC, 1 CC, 3 MC, 1 CC, 1 MC, 1 CC, 3 MC, 1 CC, 23 MC.

Row 87: 25 MC, 1 CC, 5 MC, 1 CC, 8 MC, 4 MC, 1 CC, 4 MC, 31 MC.

Row 88: 14 MC, 1 CC, 65 MC.

Row 89: 62 MC, 2 CC, 2 MC, 1 CC, 13 MC.

Row 90: 13 MC, 1 CC, 1 MC, 1 CC, 2 MC, 1 CC, 61 MC.

Row 91: 63 MC, 3 CC, 14 MC.

Row 92: 12 MC, 1 CC, 2 MC, 1 CC, 1 MC, 1 CC, 62 MC.

Row 93: 62 MC, 1 CC, 2 MC, 2 CC, 13 MC.

Row 94: 16 MC, 1 CC, 63 MC.

Chart 10

This chart is worked over 11 sts.

Row 1 (RS): 3 MC, 2 CC, 6 MC.

Row 2 (WS): 5 MC, 1 CC, 5 MC.

Row 3: 6 MC, 1 CC, 4 MC.

Row 4: (1 CC, 2 MC) × 2, 2 CC, 3 MC.

Row 5: (2 MC, 1 CC) × 2, 1 MC, 1 CC, 2 MC, 1 CC.

Row 6: 1 MC, 1 CC, 2 MC, 3 CC, 2 MC, 1 CC, 1 MC.

Row 7: 1 CC, 2 MC, 1 CC, 1 MC, (1 CC, 2 × MC) × 2.

Row 8: 3 MC, 2 CC, (2 MC, 1 CC) × 2.

Row 9: 4 MC, 1 CC, 6 MC.

Row 10: repeat row 2.

Row 11: 6 MC, 2 CC, 3 MC.

Row 12: Using MC, purl.

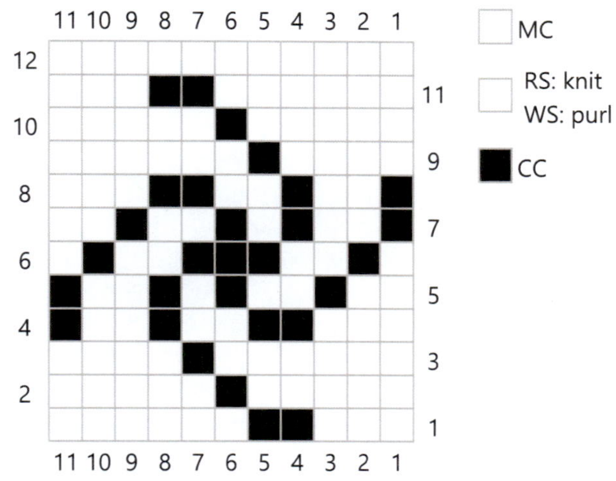

Chart 10: 6 stitches increased.

Sonar Socks

Diane Ugo

The Sonar Socks are inspired by Captain Sonar. In this cat and mouse game each team uses their tracking and evasion skills to scope out the opposing team.

The sonar had to be the main feature, it's recognisable and in this pattern it makes a great beginner texture project.

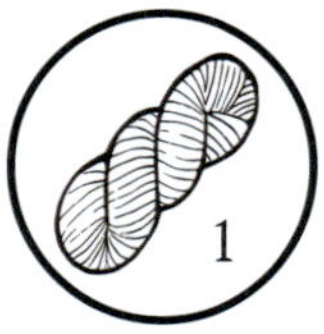

Yarn

Third Vault Yarns Librarian sock in *Undersea* 400 m / 100 g.

75% Superwash BFL 25% Nylon, 1 skein

Needles

2.25 circular needles or size to obtain gauge. Suggested 80 cm / 32″ length. Dpns or mini circs can be used if you prefer.

Notions

2 removable stitch markers which look different for bind off.

Tapestry needle

Gauge

34 sts × 46 rows to 10 cm / 4″ in Stocking stitch

Sizes

S (M, L)

Finished size (to fit approx.): 17.5(20, 23) cm / 7(8, 9)″ circumference at ball of foot.

Notes

When working the **left sock**, the BOR will change, before working from the chart. This means as you work, the heel/back of the sock will be facing you at the beginning of each round.

The toe is worked across two circular needles, labelled N1 and N2. N1 will be the top of foot/front sts and N2 the sole/heel/ back sts.

Those knitting the small size should work the stitches within the red area on the chart.

Both socks

CO 16 sts using Judy's Magic Cast On. 8 sts on each needle, pm for BOR.

Set-up (on N1): K1, m1r, k to last st, m1l, k1. Repeat on N2.

Continue increasing as set until there is a total of 32 [40,48] sts.

Toe shaping cont.

Rounds 1, 3, 5, 8, 11, 15 (N1 sts): K1, m1r, k to last st, m1l, k1. Repeat on N2.

Rounds 2, 4, 6, 7, 9, 10, 12–14: Knit all sts (N1 & N2).

Work shaping until you have 56 [64,72] sts in total.

Right sock

Knit straight for 15 [10,10] rnds and then work all rounds of Chart 1: Right Foot.

Continue in St st until 5 cm / 2″ short of foot length.

Then knit 28 [32,36], to set up to work the heel.

Heel

Heel is worked over next 28 [32,36] sts using the wrap and turn short row technique. For a deeper heel, work over 34 [38,42] sts.

First half of heel

Short Row 1: knit until the last st, sl1 wyif, turn.

SR2: Sl1 wyif, purl until the last st, sl1 wyib, turn.

SR3: Sl1 wyib, knit until 1 st before the previously wrapped st, sl1 wyif, turn.

SR4: Sl1 wyif, purl until 1 st before the previously wrapped st, sl1 wyib, turn.

Repeat rows 3 & 4 until there are 10 unwrapped stitches.

Second half of heel

SR1: k across the 10 unwrapped sts, pick up the wrap at the bottom of the next st working from the front and place it on the needle, knit the wrap together with the st, wrap the next st (as in the first half of the heel), turn.

SR2: sl the newly wrapped st, purl to the first wrapped st (on the other side of the unwrapped sts), pick up the wrap working from the back and place it on the needle, purl the wrap together with the st, wrap the next st (as in the first half of the heel), turn.

SR3: knit to the st with two wraps, pick up both wraps (as instructed in R1) and knit together with the st, wrap the next st, turn.

SR4: purl to the st with two wraps (on the other side of the unwrapped sts), pick up both wraps (as instructed in R2) and purl together with the st, wrap the next st, turn.

Repeat rows 3 & 4 until all wrapped stitches have been worked, k across N2 stitches to BOR.

Right leg

Knit 15 [10, 10] rnds straight and then work all rounds of Chart 2: Leg.

Then knit another 15 [10, 10] rnds even.

Cuff

Work in k1, p1 rib for 20 rounds.

Bind off set-up

Round 1: *k1, sl1wyif* (knit the knits and slip the purls wyif); repeat from * to * to the end.

Round 2: *sl1wyib, p1* (slip the knits wyib and purl the purls); repeat from * to * to the end.

Repeat these two rounds once more.

Tubular bind off

Cut the yarn leaving a tail that is at least four times longer than the circumference of the cuff. Thread tail onto tapestry needle.

Attach removable stitch markers, to the first two sts (1 knit and 1 purl).

Step 1: Take the tapestry needle and work it through the first st, knitwise. Take the stitch off the knitting needle but do not pull the yarn through.

Step 2: Next, ignoring the purl st, work the needle through the next knit st as if to purl. Pull the yarn all the way through.

Step 3: Work the tapestry needle through the first purl st as if to purl, take the st off the knitting needle but do not pull the yarn through.

Step 4: Working from the back and ignoring the knit st, work the tapestry needle through the next purl st as if to knit. Pull the yarn all the way through.

Repeat these four steps, until two sts remain. To help you remember:

- Knit the Knit, Off
- Ignore the Purl
- Purl the Knit and pull the yarn
- Purl the Purl, Off
- Ignore the knit
- Knit the Purl, from the back and pull the yarn

Now place the first knit st (with the stitch marker attached to it) back onto the knitting needle, working from the other end of the needle to the live sts. The right leg of the stitch should be at the front, you can use the stitch marker to lift up the stitch if it helps. Remove the stitch marker.

Do the same for the first purl stitch.

Then repeat the four steps for the BO.

Remove the knitting needle after the final step.

Weave in tail.

Left sock

Repeat CO and toe instructions for Right Sock

Knit across 14 [9, 9] rounds.

Then knit 28, [32, 36] sts (this is now the BOR).

Work from Chart 3: Left Foot.

After in the same style as for right sock, continue in St st until 5 cm/2″ short of foot length, then work from heel instructions.

Left leg

Knit 15 [10, 10] rounds straight and then work all rounds of Chart 2 (see page 5).

After knit 15 [10, 10] rnds.

Cuff

Repeat cuff instructions and then BO.

Charts

Right foot, S

Round 1: Knit (16 sts)

Round 2 and all even-numbered rounds: Knit.

Round 3: Knit.

Round 5: Knit.

Round 7: P5, k11.

Round 9: P7, k9.

Round 11: K5, p3, k8.

Round 13: P4, k3, p3, k6.

Round 15: P6, k2, p3, k5.

Round 17: K4, p3, k2, p3, k4.

Round 19: K4, p2, k2, p3, k3, p4, k3, p3, k2, p2, k4.

Round 21: K4, p2, k2, p2, k3, p6, k3, p2, k2, p2, k4.

Round 23: K4, (p2, k2) × 2, p8, (k2, p2) × 2, k4.

Round 25: Repeat round 21.

Round 27: Repeat round 19.

knit

• purl

Size S - Motif

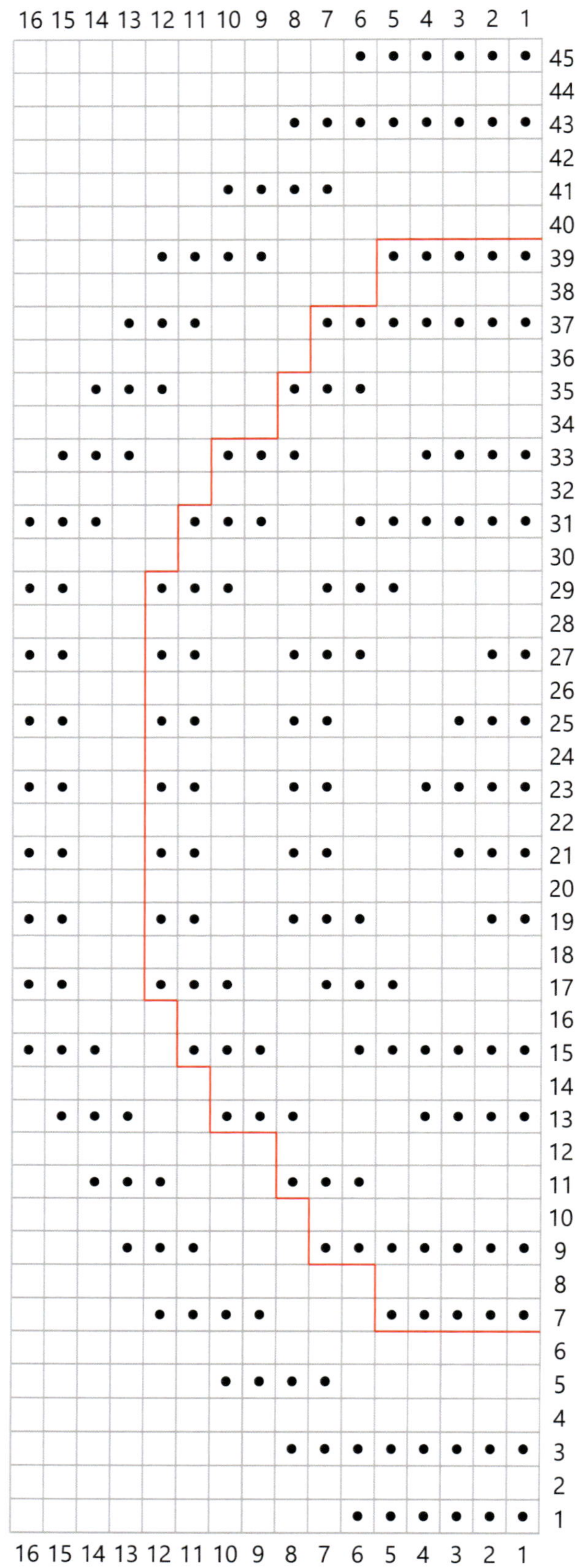

Chart 1: Right foot: k3, work chart, k to end.
Size S – motif is worked within the red area, knit all other sts.

Round 29: Repeat round 17.

Round 31: Repeat round 15.

Round 33: Repeat round 13.

Round 35: Repeat round 11.

Round 37: Repeat round 9.

Round 39: Repeat round 7.

Round 41–45: Knit.

Right foot, M/L

Round 1: P6, k10. (16 sts)

Round 2 and all even-numbered rounds: Knit.

Round 3: P8, k8.

Round 5: K6, p4, k6.

Round 7: P5, k3, p4, k4.

Round 9: P7, k3, p3, k3.

Round 11: K5, p3, k3, p3, k2.

Round 13: P4, k3, p3, k2, p3, k1.

Round 15: P6, (k2, p3) × 2.

Round 17: K4, (p3, k2) × 2, p2.

Round 19: P2, k3, p3, (k2, p2) × 2.

Round 21: P3, k3, (p2, k2) × 2, p2.

Round 23: P4, (k2, p2) × 3.

Round 25: Repeat round 21.

Round 27: Repeat round 19.

Round 29: Repeat round 17.

Round 31: Repeat round 15.

Round 33: Repeat round 13.

Round 35: Repeat round 11.

Round 37: Repeat round 9.

Round 39: Repeat round 7.

Round 41: Repeat round 5.

Round 43: P8, k8.

Round 45: P6, k10.

Leg, S

Round 1: Knit. (32 sts)

Round 2 and all even-numbered rounds: Knit.

Round 3: Knit.

Round 5: Knit.

Round 7: K11, p10, k11.

Round 9: K9, p14, k9.

Round 11: K8, p3, k10, p3, k8.

Round 13: K6, p3, k3, p8, k3, p3, k6.

Round 15: K5, p3, k2, p12, k2, p3, k5.

Round 17: K4, p3, k2, p3, k8, p3, k2, p3, k4.

Round 19: K4, p2, k2, p3, k3, p4, k3, p3, k2, p2, k4.

Round 21: K4, p2, k2, p2, k3, p6, k3, p2, k2, p2, k4.

Round 23: K4, (p2, k2) × 2, p8, (k2, p2) × 2, k4.

Round 25: Repeat round 21.

Round 27: Repeat round 19.

Round 29: Repeat round 17.

Round 31: Repeat round 15.

Round 33: Repeat round 13.

Round 35: Repeat round 11.

Round 37: Repeat round 9.

Round 39: Repeat round 7.

Round 41: Knit.

Round 43: Knit.

Round 45: Knit.

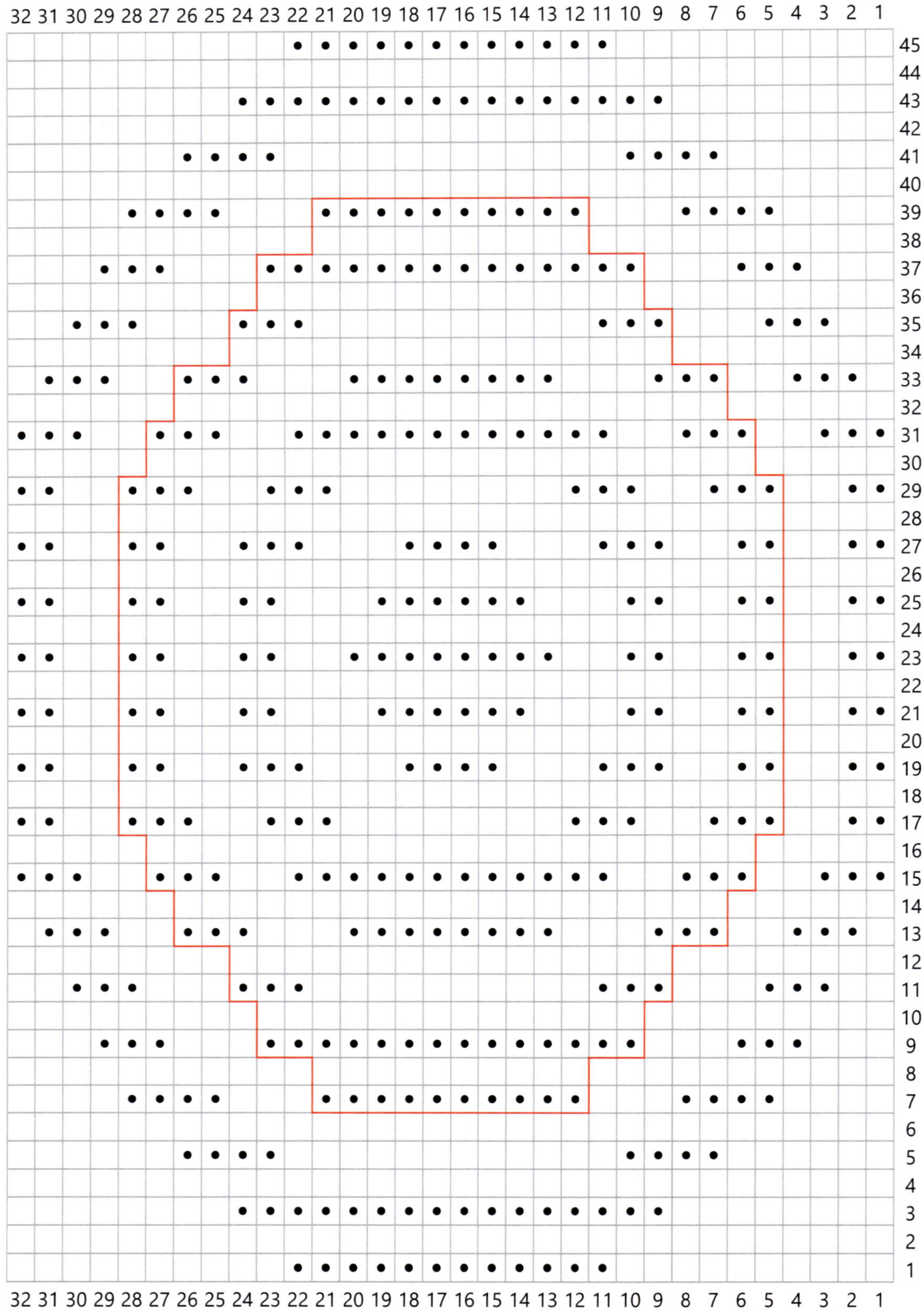

Chart 2: Leg: k13 (16, 20) work chart, knit to end.
Size S – motif is worked inside red area, knit all other sts.

knit

• purl

Size S - Motif

Leg, M/L

Round 1: K10, p12, k10. (32 sts)

Round 2 and all even-numbered rounds: Knit.

Round 3: K8, p16, k8.

Round 5: K6, p4, k12, p4, k6.

Round 7: K4, p4, k3, p10, k3, p4, k4.

Round 9: K3, p3, k3, p14, k3, p3, k3.

Round 11: K2, p3, k3, p3, k10, p3, k3, p3, k2.

Round 13: K1, p3, k2, p3, k3, p8, k3, p3, k2, p3, k1.

Round 15: (P3, k2) × 2, p12, (k2, p3) × 2.

Round 17: P2, (k2, p3) × 2, k8, (p3, k2) × 2, p2.

Round 19: (P2, k2) × 2, p3, k3, p4, k3, p3, (k2, p2) × 2.

Round 21: (P2, k2) × 2, p2, k3, p6, k3, (p2, k2) × 2, p2.

Round 23: (P2, k2) × 3, p8, (k2, p2) × 3.

Round 25: Repeat round 21.

Round 27: Repeat round 19.

Round 29: Repeat round 17.

Round 31: Repeat round 15.

Round 33: Repeat round 13.

Round 35: Repeat round 11.

Round 37: Repeat round 9.

Round 39: Repeat round 7.

Round 41: Repeat round 5.

Round 43: Repeat round 3.

Round 45: Repeat round 1.

Left foot, S

Round 1: Knit. (16 sts)

Round 2 and all even-numbered rounds: Knit.

Round 3: Knit.

Round 5: Knit.

Round 7: K11, p5.

Round 9: K9, p7.

Round 11: K8, p3, k5.

Round 13: K6, p3, k3, p4.

Round 15: K5, p3, k2, p6.

Round 17: K4, p3, k2, p3, k4.

Round 19: K4, p2, k2, p3, k3, p2.

Round 21: K4, p2, k2, p2, k3, p3.

Round 23: K4, (p2, k2) × 2, p4.

Round 25: Repeat round 21.

Round 27: Repeat round 19.

Round 29: Repeat round 17.

Round 31: Repeat round 15.

Round 33: Repeat round 13.

Round 35: Repeat round 11.

Round 37: K9, p7.

Round 39: K11, p5.

Round 41: Knit.

Round 43: Knit.

Round 45: Knit.

Left foot, M/L

Round 1: K10, p6. (16 sts)

Round 2 and all even-numbered rounds: Knit.

Round 3: K8, p8.

Round 5: K6, p4, k6.

Round 7: K4, p4, k3, p5.

Round 9: K3, p3, k3, p7.

Round 11: K2, p3, k3, p3, k5.

Round 13: K1, p3, k2, p3, k3, p4.

Round 15: (P3, k2) × 2, p6.

Round 17: P2, (k2, p3) × 2, k4.

Round 19: (P2, k2) × 2, p3, k3, p2.

Round 21: (P2, k2) × 2, p2, k3, p3.

Round 23: (P2, k2) × 3, p4.

Round 25: Repeat round 21.

Round 27: Repeat round 19.

Round 29: Repeat round 17.

Round 31: Repeat round 15.

Round 33: Repeat round 13.

Round 35: Repeat round 11.

Round 37: Repeat round 9.

Round 39: Repeat round 7.

Round 41: Repeat round 5.

Round 43: K8, p8.

Round 45: K10, p6.

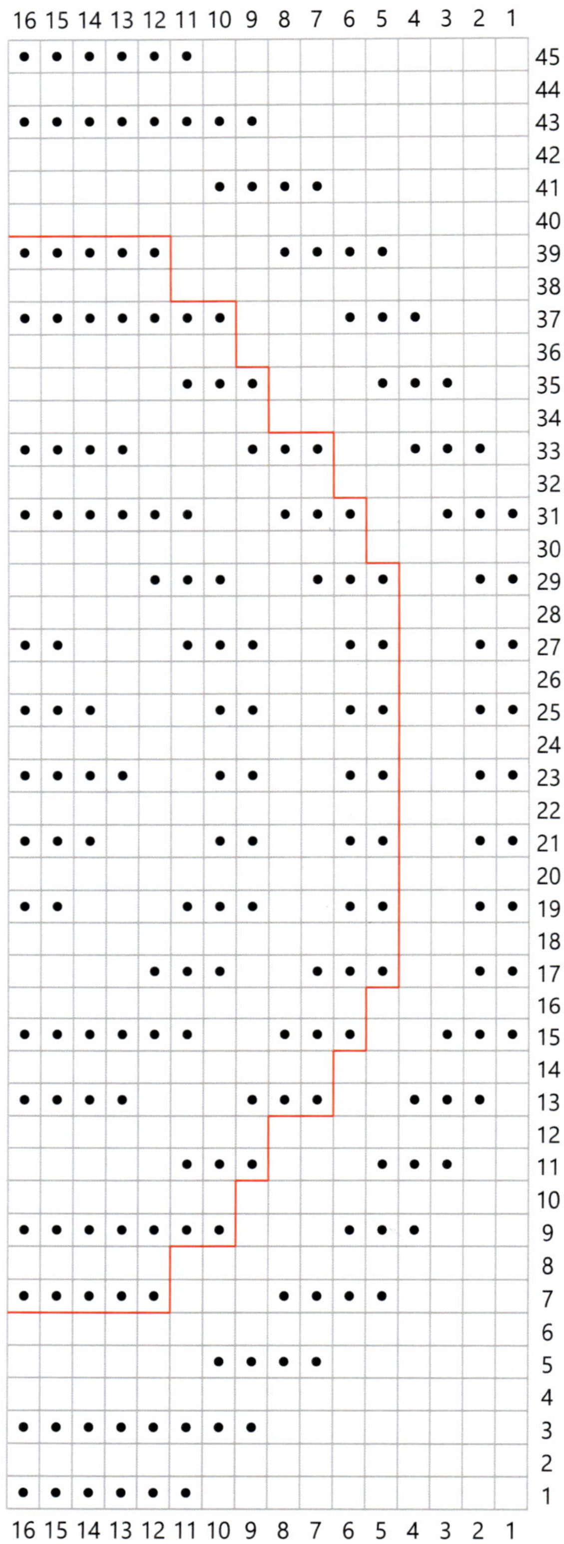

knit

purl

Size S - Motif

Chart 3: Left foot: k37 (45, 53) work from chart, k to end. *Size S – motif is worked inside red area, knit all other sts.*

Abbreviations

" inch

BO bind off

BOR beginning of round

CC contrast colour

CDD central double decrease, slip 2 stitches together knitwise as if to knit 2 together, k1, then pass slipped stitches over.

CDDP central double decrease purl, Slip 1 st off the needle, hold to front, slip next st purlwise, place held st on to right needle, p1, then pass slipped stitches over.

cm centimetres

CO cast on

DnSK drop next stitch and k1 into the topmost bar

DnSKPK drop next stitch and k1, p1, k1 into the topmost bar

DPN double pointed needle

K knit

K1 uls Knit 1 under loose strand.

k2tog knit 2 sts together

Kfb (knit into fb) Knit into front and back of same stitch.

k tbl knit through the back loop

Kpk (k1, p1, k1) in 1 stitch Knit, purl and knit into the same stitch to make 3 stitches from 1.

Kyok Knit, yarnover and knit into the same stitch to make 3 stitches from 1.

Kyokcdd (k1, yo, k1) in cdd sts, Slip 2 stitches as if to knit 2 together, k1, don't drop the st you knit into, pass slipped sts over onto your left needle, yarnover and knit through those 3 sts, then drop those sts off the left needle.

LH left hand

LLI left lifted increase: knit next stitch, then knit stitch below stitch just knitted

m metres

MC main colour

mm milimetres

m1 increase a stitch

m1l Working from the front, pick up the strand of yarn between the two sts and knit in the back of the stitch. Creates a left leaning stitch.

m1r Working from the back, pick up the strand of yarn between the two sts and knit in the front of the stitch. Creates a right leaning stitch.

m1pl Working from the front, pick up the strand of yarn between the two sts and purl through back loop. Left leaning.

m1pr Working from the back, pick up the strand of yarn between the two sts and purl in the front loop. Right leaning.

P purl

Pg page

pm place marker

p2tog purl 2 sts together

p2tog tbl purl 2 sts together through the back loop

psso pass slipped st over.

pyop p1, yo, p1 into same st

Pyopcdd (p1, yo, p1) in cdd sts, Slip 1 st off the needle, hold to front, slip next st purlwise, place held st on to right needle, p1, don't drop the st you purled into, then pass slipped

	stitches over onto your left needle, yarnover, p1 through those 3 sts, then drop those sts off the left needle.
RH	right hand
RS	right side of knitting
Rpt	repeat
Rx	row x
Skp	slip st purl wise, knit next stitch, pass slipped stitch over the knitted stitch
SK2P	slip 1 stitch, knit 2 stitches together, pass slipped stitch over the knitted stitch (2 stitches decreased)
sl1	slip 1 st purlwise, with your working yarn held at the back of the work
sl1kwise	slip 1st as if to knit
sl2 wyib	slip 2 st purlwise, with your working yarn held at the back of the work
sl2 wyif	slip 2 sts purlwise with your working yarn held in front of the work.
sm	slip marker
ssk	slip, slip, knit the two slip stitches together through the back loop.
Ssp	slip, slip, purl the two sts together
SRTC	Small size, Right Thumb chart
SLTC	Small size, Left Thumb chart
St st	stockinette stitch
St/s	stitch/es
WS	wrong side of knitting
yo	yarn over

Cable stitches

1/1 RC	Slip next stitch to cable needle and place at back of work, k1, then k1 from cable needle.
2/1 RPC	slip 1 stitch onto cable needle, hold in back, k2, p1 from cable needle
2/1 LPC	slip 2 stitches onto cable needle, hold in front, p1, k2 from cable needle

Techniques

This book is intended as a pattern collection, not a reference book. There are many great references for each technique described here so if you are unsure please look them up. The main techniques used in this book have accompanying video tutorials, which can be found on thirdvaultyarns.com, under Board Game Knits Volume 2.

Blocking

Blocking is the final touch to your project, it helps the yarn to bloom and evens out your stitches whilst opening up lace, settling cables and generally making your project shine.

To **wet block**, soak the project in lukewarm water until saturated, gently squeeze out the excess water, then pin out your project to its final dimensions and let it dry.

To **steam block**, pin out your project to its final dimensions then hold a steam iron over the project letting the steam penetrate. Never let the iron touch the project as this will flatten the stitches, and could burn or melt the yarn. Let the project dry completely before removing the pins.

Cables

Cables are a style of knitting where you cross one or a group of stitches over another, creating an almost weaved effect, as the stitches are now layered. In this book, only simple cables are used which can be completed with the aid of a third needle or cable needle to hold the stitches as you work the crossings.

Charts

Charts are a visual representation of the knitting pattern. Each square of a chart corresponds to a stitch in your work. Repeats are indicated by a coloured box and are worked as many times as stated in the written instructions. They can be used alongside the written pattern, and make sure that if you use them that you always refer to the chart notes and the key before you begin.

Colourwork

Intarsia

This method of colourwork knitting uses one colour at a time to create separate blocks of colour. Each colour is picked up and knit, then put down to pick up the next colour. It is joined together by wrapping the strand of new working yarn around the previous colour working yarn, whenever a change between colours occurs.

Stranded knitting

Also called Fair Isle, this method uses two or more colours of yarn at a time to create multicoloured patterns whilst knitting. The yarns are carried across the work, and the colour not in use is carried loosely behind the work, and captured every 4 or so stitches, creating floats. Keep all floats very loose to maintain elasticity and reduce any pulling in of the project. It is also important to consider colour dominance, as the yarn that is carried underneath the other/s will show as the most prominent in the project. Keep this consistent for the duration of your project.

Drop stitches

Drop stitch patterning is a type of lace where the pattern will utilise strategic placement of single closed-off drop stitches or finite ladders of dropped stitches to create lace openwork.

Duplicate stitch

Also called Swiss darning, this is a decorative stitch that is sewn over stockinette knitting by following the legs of each knitted stitch, it can be used to add motifs or designs to your knitting after the item is already completed.

It is recommended that you either use the same type of yarn for duplicate stitch as you used in your project, just in a different colour, or use a slightly thicker yarn as this will cover the stitches below properly and ensure that the other colour does not show through.

Grafting

Also known as Kitchener stitch, this is a technique that is used to seamlessly join two rows of live stitches, forming what is essentially a new row between them.

Lace bind off

Often called Russian bind off, this creates a stable but very elastic edge, most commonly used on lace shawls when they will be blocked out with points. It is worked by either knitting or purling two stitches then slipping the two worked stitches back onto the other needle and either knitting or purling them together. Knit or purl one more stitch then slip the two worked stitches and work them as previous. Continue like this until you reach your last stitch, cut the working yarn and pull it through.

Lateral braid

A lateral braid is a horizontal column of knitting on top of a vertical knitted piece. It is knit at the same time as the row below it, by creating an extra stitch at the beginning and then constantly slipping and using a technique similar to cabling, to carry and knit stitches that grow from the created stitch as you continue along the row.

Long tail cast on

This cast on creates an elastic edge that is perfect for anything that needs stretch, 1 × 1 rib included. There are a few different methods that show you how to create the best long tail cast on for the knitting you will do after, plain knitting, ribbing and more. Please use the one that you are most comfortable with.

Tubular cast on and off

This stretchy cast on method creates what appears to be a seamless rounded hem to your knitting, replacing the typical cast on with another row of stitches. The same effect is created when using this method of bind off. The Tubular cast off is described in the Sonar Socks pattern.

Seams

Seams are structural join between two pieces of knitted fabric. In this book they are used to join the sides of the Mind Reaper Mitts. It is recommended you use mattress stitch for seaming as it is simple and provides a join that looks seamless. For information on different seaming techniques, the Vogue knitting website is a great resource.

Short rows

To work short rows, you knit part of the way through a row, then stop and turn the work around before the end and work back over the stitches you just knit. The method used in these patterns is the German short row method that uses the creation of a double stitch at your turning point to close holes created by turning mid row.

Stretchy bind off

There are many different types of stretchy bind off, the only thing they have in common is creating vary degrees of elasticity in a finished edge. Some are tailored to different types of knitting so it is worth choosing the one you use with an eye to what you have made. As with everything you will find it easiest to use your preferred method.

Yarn glossary

Third Vault Yarns

Tesseract

55% Superwash Bluefaced Leicester 45% Silk

Heavy Laceweight / Light fingering weight 600 m/100 g

A finely spun 2 plied yarn that has sheen and lots of drape from the silk, whilst retaining some structure from the wool. Try a Tencel blend as an alternative to maintain drape, if not a wool silk blend.

Companion 4ply | Shawl

100% Superwash Merino

Fingering weight 400 m/100 g | 600 m/150 g

Tightly spun 4 plied smooth soft yarn, that has good stretch and bounce, whilst maintaining decent drape. A good substitute would be a wool that has much the same properties, rougher wools are not recommended. Non-wool blends or yarn would work for the shawls, but not the mitts due to lack of elasticity.

Caroline Dk

100% Superwash Merino

Double knitting weight 230 m/115 g

Smoothly 4 plied, very springy bouncy yarn, with a put up similar to a light worsted weight, can substitute this with a worsted weight or a Standard Dk. When substituting look for a wool that has good stretch and bounce. The hat pattern can also be made in a cotton, however be mindful that there will be less stretch.

Librarian Sock

75% Superwash Bluefaced Leicester 25% nylon

Sock weight 425 m/100 g

Tightly spun 4 plied yarn, with a robustness from the BFL wool used with nylon added for more strength. When substituting any sock wool can be used, containing nylon for longevity. It is recommended to choose a hardier wool than merino for socks.

Gamercrafting

Merino Dk Minis

100% Superwash Merino Dk

Double knitting weight 42 m/20 g

12 plied smooth and springy Dk wool yarn, similar to many commercial brands of Dk wool, alternatives are fairly accessible in a range of prices.

Truly Hooked

Standard Sock | Minis

75% Superwash merino, 25% nylon

Sock weight 425 m / 100 g | 82 m / 20 g

Soft and tightly spun 4 plied yarn, can be substituted with any sock yarn containing nylon for strength and durability. Wool fibres are suggested for comfort and stretch.

John Arbon Textiles

Yarnadelic Sport

100% Corriedale

Sport weight 333 m / 100 g

A rounded 3 plied yarn, with softness, bounce and lustre, created to provide great stitch definition and drape. When substituting any sport or 4ply weight yarn can be used, however choices should focus on yarns that would provide high stitch definition.

Exmoor Sock

60% Exmoor Blueface superwash, 20% Corriedale superwash, 10% Zwartbles, 10% Nylon

4ply weight 400 m / 100 g

A smooth higher twist, 3 plied sock yarn, that is made of a blend of different fibres to add robustness, bounce, softness and lustre with some nylon for added durability. Any smooth wool sock yarns can be substituted for this, for the same feel choose other lambswools, with nylon if using for socks. Though for the cowl, nylon is not necessary. A yarn with good elasticity and ability to hold its shape is recommended for structure.